Things to Do When You Turn 21

Published by Sellers Publishing, Inc.

161 John Roberts Road, South Portland, Maine 04106

www.sellerspublishing.com • E-mail: rsp@rsvp.com

Mary L. Baldwin, Managing Editor
Project Editor, Elisabeth Vincentelli
Production Editor, Charlotte Cromwell

Cover Design by Mary L. Baldwin
Interior Design by Charlotte Cromwell

ISBN 13: 978-1-4162-4633-6

Library of Congress Control Number: 2017931646

10 9 8 7 6 5 4 3 2 1

Printed in the United States of America.

Credits: Page 224

MAKING THE MOST OF YOUR MILESTONE BIRTHDAY

Things to Do When You Turn 21

EDITED BY RONNIE SELLERS

Commissioning Editor: Elisabeth Vincentelli

SELLERS
PUBLISHING

Contents

Introduction

Congratulations. You have reached an important milestone in your life. You have survived the angst of adolescence, persevered through the ups and downs of your teenage years, endured countless lectures and unsolicited opinions from your elders, and you've managed to come through it all without losing your sense of yourself or your optimism about your future. Hats off to you!

I've often heard it said that today's young adults are far more savvy and sophisticated than those of previous generations. I think this is, for the most part, bunk, and I question how important it is to be "savvy and sophisticated" anyway. I've met many people who are considered to be savvy and sophisticated by their peers. All too often I've found that "savvy and sophisticated" really means "ruthless and condescending." In other words, people you would be better off avoiding.

It is hard to deny, however, that turning 21 in the age of the internet, social media, virtual reality and artificial intelligence requires navigating through a world that's far more complex, and changing at a faster pace, than the one your parents encountered when they were your age.

Sure, some things haven't changed. For instance, one of the greatest ironies of all time, as far as I'm concerned, still persists. In the USA, at age 18, you can go into a voting booth and cast a vote to help decide who will be empowered to launch a nuclear bomb. However, you still cannot, in most states, walk into a bar and order a shot until you turn 21. Think about that for a moment. Doesn't it seem like it should be the other way around?

But now you are 21, so if you do live in the USA, or in most other countries, you can both order a shot AND cast your vote. This is very fortunate, because these days you may very well need a strong shot before heading into the voting booth . . . and another after the results are made public!

While I'm sure it is gratifying to finally have a voice in what happens politically, it is likely that your primary concern is figuring out what you're going to do with the rest of your life. You've probably already realized that your time is a finite, and precious, commodity. You can't make more of it. You can only get smarter about what you do with it. And the number of publishers, broadcasters, Web sites, apps, and entertainment providers vying for your time increases every day.

Today's media, when reporting on your peer group, often spotlights business whiz kids who have become millionaires before turning 21. The internet has, without question, made it possible for young people to access information and develop skills that their parents and grandparents didn't get or develop until they were much older, if at all. In some cases, members of the up-and-coming generation have put the information and programming skill they acquired on-line to use to start companies like Facebook and Oculus and Tumblr, and those companies have, indeed, made their founders extremely wealthy.

Psychologists have long agreed, however, that beyond a certain point there is little correlation between wealth and happiness. Obviously, it's difficult to feel happiness in a sustained way if you don't have enough money to cover your basic needs. But research has shown that once a certain level of financial security is reached, more money doesn't ensure more happiness.

If money won't make you happy, then what will? What can you do now, at age 21, to begin to build a life that will be fulfilling and meaningful and rewarding?

This is the question we hoped to shed some light on when we began planning this book. We realized at the outset that if we wanted the book to be relevant to your generation we should reach out to people who are close enough to you in age to remember their experiences of turning 21, and, therefore, be familiar with the world in which you must operate.

We were very fortunate to find 21 thoughtful and erudite contributors from different backgrounds and professional disciplines to offer their perspectives on the subject of finding success and happiness in life. They are not, for the most part, millionaires, but each of them has followed his or her own path and, by doing so, learned some important lessons about what is important in life . . . and (just as important) what is not.

They were also generous enough to take the time to share their insights, experiences and advice aobut the experience of turing 21 with our editor, Elisabeth Vincentelli. The result is a comprehensive, diverse, and often humorous compendium on the subject, one that I hope you will find useful and uplifting as you begin the exciting process of creating your own rewarding and happy life.

Ronnie Sellers, Publisher

Don't worry about proving yourself

Anna Chlumsky

Emmy® Nominated "Veep" Actress

For many child actors, moving into an adult career can be difficult. **ANNA CHLUMSKY** is an example of how to successfully handle that transition. She first became famous when she starred opposite Macaulay Culkin in the 1991 movie *My Girl*. But instead of trying to pursue acting, she stuck with school and majored in International Studies at the University of Chicago. After graduation she worked in publishing, and eventually decided to return to performance. She enrolled at the Atlantic Acting School and landed small parts on TV and in Off Broadway shows, before signing up for the role of Amy Brookheimer on HBO's hit series *Veep* — a part that has earned her four consecutive Emmy nominations for Outstanding Supporting Actress in a Comedy Series. She made her Broadway debut in 2015 in *You Can't Take It with You*. Now 36, Chlumsky lives in Brooklyn, NY, with her husband.

Q Did you have a role model growing up? If yes, who was it and why?

A The women in my stepmother's family were my favorite women growing up. Grandma Fiorito had seven kids. She was an expert on family, and she never hesitated to give you her mind. I loved that about her. She was fearless and no-bullshit. My Auntie Carla to this day is the woman I keep in my head when I think of the mother I want to be. Growing up, she was always so cool-headed, honest, funny, and it was always so remarkable to me how she carried herself. Like a whole person. She loves my cousins with all her might, but without that achy need-trap so many mothers can fall into. Auntie Googie is a trip. She's loud, speaks her mind, and we love her for it. Of course, everyone's got their days, and none of these women are perfect by any means. But with the Fiorito women, I've always gotten the sense that they were fine with their imperfections and knew they were worthy all the same. It's a beautiful thing, this feminine confidence. I love them so much for it and aspire to embody the same steadfastness in my own womanhood.

Q Who influenced you in your early life?

A My mother. It was just her and me growing up, so we sort of lived and breathed each other in my very early years.

Q What illuminating, instructive and/or inspirational thoughts can you share that reflect your perspective on that time of your life?

A Kids are people. They want to be treated as people. They may not have the experience of older kids or adults, but their emotions and thoughts are just as complex and sophisticated. So, while young people aren't ready for certain adult situations or concepts, they can certainly feel everything around them, and they don't miss a beat. Do not condescend and do not assume they can't keep up. Stephen Sondheim nailed it on the head, "Careful the things you say. Children will listen." Word.

Q What was your biggest challenge or biggest break in your early life that led you to where you are today?

A A movie called *My Girl*. Everything is defined as before and after that thing.

Q Looking back, what motivated you to get to where you are now?

A I'm motivated by the need to contribute. I'm not comfortable just taking up space. It's true, we've all already earned our place on this rock, but I feel this desperate need to make the most of it while I'm here. I do believe that anyone who is alive at any given moment is a steward of the planet. It's a privilege to be so. So I strive to honor that privilege.

Q **What were your dreams in your late teens or early twenties?**

A To be great at something. Truly great. Or at the very least, to aspire to greatness.

Q **Could you picture what you would end up doing?**

A I knew it wouldn't be "ordinary" in the sense of clocking in somewhere and collecting a pension at retirement. I knew I'd incur adventure and creativity somewhere. How would I get there? My ideas ran the gamut from collecting fish specimens in the Amazon to being an interpreter for the UN to training race horses to acting on Broadway. It was all possible.

Q **When did you first realize you were good at what you do now?**

A The first day of scene study at the Atlantic Acting School when I was 24. I thought, "Well, I'm giving this acting thing a shot, and if I like it I'll continue." Then, that first day of scene study — taking a scene, analyzing your character's actions, applying moment-to-moment exercises — it was just all so fun. I was in. For life. Honestly, I don't even know if I felt "good" at it. It just felt so good. I just loved doing it, and I believed that if I enjoyed it, I must be good at it, too. Or I'd get there eventually.

Q Were your family encouraging?

A My family has a showbiz lineage, so I was lucky in that I never had to convince anyone that this path was worth pursuing. Everyone I knew already got it.

Q A lot of people say high school or college was a turning point. Did you feel that way?

A College was a huge turning point for me as a person. It was the first place I went where just thinking, learning, putting together an intelligent thought were enough. I was finally good enough. I finally felt worthy. After an adolescence full of rejection based on things beyond my control, (looks, weight, age, marketability, etc.), I finally felt like I belonged somewhere and that I was accepted for who I was. And for whom I was becoming. I felt safe for the first time in a very long time.

Q Do you have a favorite quote or mantra that keeps you going?

A The angels write it better than I can. Also, *Deus escreve* *certo por linhas tortas* — God writes straight in crooked lines.

Q **What lesson have you learned over the years that has stuck with you?**

A I truly believe that the essence of all philosophy and religion are asking us to say, "I don't know." It is our duty to pursue knowledge, but we must also accept that the more we know, the more mysteries we uncover. Also, while life is certainly complex, and nothing is ever black and white, I do think most decisions can be distilled down to love vs. fear. The "love" path will always be the right one.

Q **What advice would you tell your 21-year-old self, knowing what you know now?**

A You don't have to prove anything to anyone. And be not afraid.

" I knew I'd incur adventure and creativity somewhere. How would I get there? My ideas ran the gamut from collecting fish specimens in the Amazon to being an interpreter for the UN to training race horses to acting on Broadway. It was all possible. "

Anna Chlumsky

Surround yourself with inspirational people

Christopher Gray

App Developer

When we talked to **CHRISTOPHER GRAY**, he was merely 25 and had landed on both Forbes' "30 Under 30" list and Oprah Winfrey's "SuperSoul 100" tribute to "awakened leaders." The reason: Gray created Scholly, a wildly successful app that matches hopeful students with college scholarships. Gray found out the hard way there was a need when he spent countless hours trying to find ways to pay for his education without getting in debt. He ended up raising enough money — and then some — to fully fund his studies at Drexel University. In February 2015, he appeared on TV's *Shark Tank* and earned the near-instant support of entrepreneurs Lori Greiner and Daymond John, who pledged $40,000 to help fund Gray's app in exchange for a 15% equity. From then on, Scholly was launched.

Q Can you tell us a bit about how you had the idea for Scholly?

A I'm originally from Birmingham, Alabama, and I was going to college at the peak of the recession, around 2009. My mom lost her job, a lot of people in my family lost their jobs, and a lot of schools wouldn't give me a lot of aid, so I was forced to rely on scholarships to pay for college. It took me about seven months to find all these different scholarships. I went to the library, on websites. Long story short: I ended up winning $1.3 million in scholarships. Even though it was a success story in the end, it was a tragedy just trying to find it all.

Q And you did all that on your own?

A Yes. When I went to college I started to help out other people who were coming to me. I realized there's all this money, hundreds of millions of dollars, looking for students and students looking for money, and they can't find each other. So I created Scholly, an app that turns months of looking into scholarships into minutes.

Q **Were you also concerned with kids getting burdened with loans?**

A Exactly. A lot of students take loans and when they graduate they can't find jobs, they can't buy houses, they can't do anything because they're starting off in debt. They're not aware of all the money that's out there for them, and they end up in a really bad situation when a lot of them don't have to.

Q **Did you have a lightbulb moment about what you wanted to do?**

A I was very good at finding a bunch scholarships, and I wanted to turn that skill, or that ability, into a product. I could not just help a lot of people but also create a sustainable business. We've helped students raise almost $75 million in less than two years. There are a lot of nonprofits that have been doing the same work for 25 years that haven't done that. So the lightbulb moment was realizing I could help a lot of people, create a business and use my own experiences to come full circle. Now we're helping students across the nation so they don't have the experience that I had. It's a personal crusade for me to help students who are like myself not to take out loans.

Q **Did you have a mentor or someone who was key in your growth as a person and an entrepreneur?**

A When I started college, I had a cool mentor. Actually she was my AP Literature teacher, her name was Ms. [Tara] Tidwell, and she helped me with every scholarship application I did, she encouraged me. It was a really helpful process. And I also have a mentor on the business side, Josh Kopelman from First Round Capital — they're one of the biggest venture capitalists in the world. He's one of my first investors and he wrote me a $100,000 check after a 15-minute conversation when I was just starting.

Q **Was that connected to *Shark Tank*?**

A It was a different thing. We had a *USA Today* article that came out and a [*Shark Tank*] producer reached out to us. When I think of *Shark Tank*, I think more of physical products, mom-and-pop kind of stuff. But the producer got on the phone, loved the story and asked me to come in on an audition date. A few weeks later we got a call from ABC that we got on the show. I was flown out to L.A. and I filmed for over an hour, and you saw seven minutes of that [*laughs*]. It was a great experience because I got a deal really quickly from both Lori Greiner and Daymond John — no one set them up. We were the

No. 1 app for iPhone and Android for a month. Our site was getting 9,000 hits per second. It was just incredibly absurd [*laughs*]. And I was still in college, actually. I was trying to balance all that with taking five classes. I remember being super-excited and super-nervous. I filmed but you never know how you're going to appear on TV. It was an amazing, surreal experience for us. That moment changed my life because my company was seen by millions of people in America. It was a really good experience and so much came from that. Do you watch *Grey's Anatomy*?

Q **I do!**

A Do you know Jesse Williams? He plays Dr. Jackson Avery. He's on our team now. We met at Oprah's brunch [for the "SuperSoul 100"]. We started talking and he's now a brand ambassador and board member.

Q **Was your family encouraging?**

A I went to college in Philadelphia, they're from Birmingham — I'm the first from my family to go to college and graduate. So it's a really big deal for that to happen for my family. Until that point they support you, they love you, but in a lot of ways they don't know how to support you in the best way — they never went to college, they didn't know how to navigate that process, but they made sure I had a mentor and people to help me.

Q Do you feel that now you have a responsibility as a role model in your family?

A Oh yes. I have a brother and sister who are seven and nine. They were two and three when I was going to college, so they're effectively my children in a lot of ways. It's very interesting to have that happen. It's been a very enlightening experience with them. I tell everyone that I feel like I really broke a cycle of poverty.

Q Is there a lesson that has stuck with you over the years?

A I feel that you're the average of everyone you spend most of your time with. I feel that my life is about being with like-minded and inspirational people motivating me and encouraging me. Without these people I wouldn't have learned the way I did. I believe the people around you, whether it's someone you're dating, your friends, your mentors, your co-workers, are all important in your journey: You cannot do it by yourself. These people determine how you grow, the things you learn. If you're around great people, that's good [*laughs*].

Q If you had to give your 21-year-old self a piece of advice, what would it be?

A When you're young, you think you know everything. What would have been really good for me would have been to surround myself with professional advisers early on. Growing up, I guess I wasn't exposed because I was from such a small town, but I wish I had been aware of all the free resources out there. A lot of students who are poor don't even know there are so many freebies online, etc. You're not even aware they exist. That's kind of part of my personal mission: Scholly's motto is "Opportunity for all." I want to make sure I can help as many people as possible. I'm learning and that's something I want to embrace, so I want to surround myself with really smart people to help me grow in that way.

❝So the lightbulb moment was realizing I could help a lot of people, create a business and use my own experiences to come full circle.**❞**

Christopher Gray

Find your happy and share it with others

Mayim Bialik

Emmy® Award Winning Actress

MAYIM BIALIK was 15 when she started working on *Blossom*, a successful sitcom that ran on NBC for five seasons, starting in 1990. This kind of fame is not easy to take, but Bialik handled it with poise and grace. Instead of pursuing more acting gigs when the show ended, she enrolled at UCLA, where she majored in neuroscience. She would go on to earn a Ph.D in that field, also from UCLA. This may have constituted research of sorts for the role of Dr. Amy Farrah Fowler, a neurobiologist on an even bigger TV hit, *The Big Bang Theory*, which Bialik joined in 2010. Now 41, the tireless Bialik is also the founder of the website GrokNation, which presents issues in "an accessible, relatable and unapologetically nerdy way," and the author of the 2014 cookbook *Mayim's Vegan Table*.

Q What advice would you give your 21-year-old self?

A Oh my goodness, girl! Your gut instinct is always right. With men, with the way you are treated, with things you need to speak up about. Trust your gut!

Q What talent or passion have you been able to use in your career in an unexpected way?

A What a great question. I think my underlying passion is trying to find a sense of purpose in my life no matter what I do. While I love being an entertainer, I am constantly driven by the need to find why the universe has given me the opportunities I have and how I can use those to be a positive influence in my family, in my community, and hopefully for the world at large in some way!

Q What is the one thing that influenced your career today?

A I think the one thing that influenced my career today is that there has always been someone who believes in me more than I believed in myself. First it was my mother, then it was the creator of *Blossom*, Don Reo. Then it was my biology tutor in high school, then it was Nancy Wayne, a neuroendocrinologist at UCLA, then it was my manager Tiffany Kuzon, and lastly, it has been my guardian angel best friend, a man who has become my creative and business partner, Immanuel Shalev. Those are the people who literally got me here and keep me remembering that I am on the right path.

Q **What does "finding your happy" mean to you? Do you feel you've "found it"?**

A I feel like the second I feel like I have found it, it will slip out of my hands. Finding my happy is a constant journey of always looking forward and finding ways to share with others.

Q **Prized possession?**

A The wisdom of my ancestors

"Trust your gut."

Mayim Bialik

Love the process regardless of the outcome

Emily McDowell
Louie® Award Winning Illustrator

When she was 24, **EMILY McDOWELL** was diagnosed with stage 3 Hodgkin Lymphoma. As she went through chemotherapy, the good-humored illustrator couldn't help finding inadvertent levity in receiving cards that urged her to "get well soon." In May 2013, after a close friend died of cancer and with her own cancer in remission, McDowell started her own card company out of her bedroom. The breakthrough came quickly, when a card encapsulating McDowell's offbeat, warm sensibility hit a nerve: She sold 1,700 of them in a week and it's still in her catalogue, under the name "awkward dating card."

Now 42, the Los Angeles-based McDowell continues to run her booming business, and in 2017 she co-authored the illustrated book *There Is No Good Card for This: What to Say and Do When Life Is Scary, Awful, And Unfair to People You Love* (HarperOne) with empathy expert Kelsey Crowe.

Q Who or what influenced you in your early life?

A When I was in middle and high school, I was part of
a nondenominational church youth group. It wasn't
religious in a traditional way, but it was spiritual in that
it taught us emotional literacy and how to not be awful
to each other. I feel so lucky that I was able to learn how
to talk about feelings at that point in my life, and the
woman who ran that youth group was like a parent to me.
She made me feel seen, heard, and understood when I
desperately needed it.

Q What was turning 21 like?

A Despite sitting and pondering this for hours, I have zero
memory of my actual 21st birthday. It happened 20
years ago, the summer before my senior year of college. I
remembered some of my friends' 21st birthdays, though,
so I sent a group text to six of my closest college friends:
"I'm writing a piece about turning 21, which is awkward,
because I have no recollection of this event. Did we have a
party?"

One friend said she thought we did something low-key, like have dinner at the pizza place where I worked. This was definitely not it. You don't have a 21st birthday dinner at the place where you eat free pizza five nights a week.

"Was your birthday the one where Tim was high on coke and spent all day cooking a rabbit stew? I remember that was someone's birthday, and I think it was a girl."

Nope. Although I do remember that dinner. First and last time I've eaten rabbit.

"Did we go to Cannon's?"

"What's Cannon's?"

"Oh, my bad, that's a bar on the lower east side." (Of Manhattan. We went to college in Minnesota.)

After two hours, none of us could conclusively remember my birthday, although we did ultimately remember the name of the guy who lived in our basement for a month that summer (Josh Tweed). You know, valuable information.

I share this story because it leads into my answer to the next question:

Q **What illuminating, instructive or inspirational thoughts can you share that reflect your perspective on that time of your life?**

A In my early twenties, I felt a ton of anxiety and self-imposed pressure around providing an immediate answer to the question of what I was supposed to be doing with my life. Everything felt high-stakes and important, and every decision felt monumental. And yet, here I am 20 years later, and I literally have no memory of my 21st birthday.

I think most of us assume, when we're starting out, that growing up is about figuring out what you want to do and who you want to be. But I think that in practice, it's actually the opposite: The process is a continuous refinement of learning what you don't want. The way to figure out what you do want is by navigating the vast world of Things That Are Wrong For You, crossing those things off your list, and carving smaller and smaller circles around yourself until you end up in a place that makes sense. For most of us, this process takes a long time, and to make it more complicated, most of us want different things at 21 than we do at 41.

Q **Could you picture what you would end up doing?**

A Not at all. When I graduated from college, the concept of being an entrepreneur wasn't anywhere in my consciousness. I was an English major, and when my original dream of moving to New York and working as an editorial assistant fell apart — due to the fact that I didn't have parental funding or the willingness to get a second job waiting tables to afford to live — I didn't really have a Plan B. I feel like I was only aware of the existence of a handful of jobs, and they were all established things like doctor, lawyer, editor, teacher. It took until I was 35 for me to be able to understand that I could have my own business.

Q A lot of people say high school or college was a turning point. Did you feel that way?

A Neither was a turning point for me. I always liked school, and I was good at it, but I played it safe and didn't really push myself, and I didn't take advantage of it the way some kids did. For example, I went to this great liberal arts college with a million fascinating classes, and I just kept taking the same stuff I took in high school. I took German all through high school, so when it came time to sign up for college classes, I just kept going with it. I didn't even stop to think about why, or if I wanted to keep learning German, or whether being fluent in German would be useful or relevant in any kind of future life I might have. Which meant that the second week of school junior year, sitting in my advanced German literature class, I realized for the first time: "What the hell am I doing here? I could be taking art right now." I dropped the class and completed a whole art minor in two years. I think what I'm getting at here is that it took me a while to reach my turning point.

Q Do you have a favorite quote or mantra that keeps you going?

A "Success is going from failure to failure with no loss of enthusiasm." In other words: happiness is about loving the process, regardless of the outcome. (This quote is often attributed to Winston Churchill, but apparently this is false, and nobody knows where it originated.)

Q What advice would you tell your 21-year-old self, knowing what you know now?

A You don't have to prove anything to anyone, and you don't have to impress anyone, in order to be a worthy human being. Now, with this in mind, think about what you want to do with your life. Start with what you love to do when you're by yourself. Spoiler alert: the things you hate about yourself will eventually become what strangers most like about you.

Q **What would you tell someone about to turn 21, based on your experience?**

A There is no such thing as failure: there is only learning. Sometimes you learn what you don't want. Sometimes you learn ways to do things differently. Sometimes you learn how to survive disappointment — and that you can survive disappointment, which is probably the most important skill to have. It's impossible to see the future or the whole picture from where you're standing, and sometimes not getting what you want will turn out to be the best thing that ever happened to you. Never beat yourself up for "wasting" time going in a direction that you end up abandoning. Driving down the wrong streets gives you the lay of the land, and that knowledge is always useful later.

"There is no such thing as failure: there is only learning.**"**

Emily McDowell

Learn to love what must be done

Kelly Evans

CNBC Business Anchor

KELLY EVANS had barely entered her twenties when she joined *The Wall Street Journal* as an economics reporter, not long after graduating summa cum laude from Washington and Lee University, in Virginia. The famous newspaper turned out to be a good fit and soon she was a financial columnist, as well as the host of the video segment NewsHub. She joined CNBC in 2012 as an on-air correspondent, co-anchoring the London-based *Worldwide Exchange* before moving to homebase in New York for *Squawk on the Street*. Now 32, Evans helps steer the afternoon show *Closing Bell*, where she succeeded the equally impressive Maria Bartiromo. Evans clearly holds her own on the floor of the New York Stock Exchange. Where she will go next?

Q **Did you have a role model growing up? If yes, who was it and why?**

A When I was younger, I wanted to be a celebrity and couldn't wait to get away from my parents. By my mid-twenties, I couldn't wait to get away from celebrities and wished I were more like my parents.

Q **Who or what influenced you in your early life?**

A There were a couple of teachers who played a major role in helping me feel calm and comfortable about who I was when I couldn't handle the intense social pressure of middle school in particular. My fourth-grade teacher, Ms. Novak, made being weird seem cool. My sixth-grade teacher, Mrs. Hoeft, let a friend and me bop around in her classroom during lunch instead of having to deal with the nightmare of the cafeteria.

Q **What was your biggest challenge or biggest break in your early life that led you to where you are today?**

A I went to college in the little town where I grew up, so I was eager to get away into bigger cities whenever I could.

I fortunately landed an internship at Bank of America's headquarters in Charlotte after my sophomore year that introduced me to the world of banking, business journalism, and financial markets. I loved it, and came away with experience that gave me a tremendous edge in applying for news internships the following summer, having now realized I wanted to be a business journalist. That specialization then helped me get a spot on the economics team at Reuters after my junior year and ultimately prepared me for the post-grad internship that led me to my job at *The Wall Street Journal* shortly after I graduated.

Q Looking back, what motivated you to get to where you are now?

A I grew up feeling very sheltered and bursting with ambition to go out and make a name and a career and a living for myself. As I've gotten older, I've come to appreciate our strict upbringing much more and to be wary whenever I think my ambition is getting the better of me.

Q What were your dreams in your late teens?

A Separate from wanting to be "famous," I cherished this ideal image of college as a leafy, bookish place where I'd happily spend hours studying and in class, soaking up knowledge and absorbing my professors' wisdom. It turned out for me to be a crash course in all the socializing I'd tried for so long to avoid. I am glad for that now, actually, although of course I wish I'd been more studious at the same time. I now wish I had been a history major! I have been reading furiously since after I graduated now that I've realized I actually know very little about the world.

Q Could you picture what you would end up doing, or not at all?

A I never took a journalism class until college. I dabbled a little before that by writing for my local paper, and writing had always been a passion. But I will never forget the shock upon showing up for my ten-year high school reunion, where one of our yearbooks lay open. When asked as a senior where I saw myself in 20 years, I had answered: hosting a daily national news show, then retiring to teach. I was so floored by that (since I had become, yes, host of a daily national news show) my pulse began racing. I don't know if I put it down as a joke, or in a serious way. Either way, it revealed something deeper than I knew about myself at the time!

Q When did you first realize you were into/good at what you do now?

A I remember working as a print reporter, casually watching

CNBC on the televisions in the newsroom, and thinking to myself I could do that. Of course, once I actually had the job I realized how hard it is, and how woefully unprepared I was for it. And it's been a scramble to learn how to do it, and do it well, ever since.

Q **Were your family and/or friends encouraging?**

A My parents have watched nearly every moment I have ever appeared on television (or a streaming web show), and probably read almost everything I've ever written. There have been many times when one of their simple emails saying they liked this or that aspect of the show or an interview has helped shore up my confidence when it was running perilously low. And I love my friends because we all interact the same way today as we did in high school or college, just as grown-up versions of ourselves, now raising our own families.

Q **What was school like? A lot of people say high school or college was a turning point. Did you feel that way?**

A I had been bright as a young kid but never developed strong study habits. By late high school and into college I felt the subject matter overwhelming me, and my plate was overloaded with extracurriculars like sports and, later, journalism. I really lost myself by the time I had graduated college. Work was my savior. I loved it, I was pretty good at it, I didn't mind it consuming my waking hours (at least for a while), and it ultimately drove me to the point of rediscovering myself.

Q **Describe your experience(s) turning 21.**

A I remember it well: the summer I lived in Washington, D.C., after my junior year. I was dreading the date, not being a big drinker or feeling all that great about myself at the time or wanting the commensurate attention. My good friend came to stay with me, and so we half-heartedly went bar-hopping. At the end of the evening we came back home, she promptly fell asleep, and I ate the entire Domino's pizza we had just ordered by myself. It is not a pleasant memory!

Q **Do you have a favorite quote or mantra that keeps you going?**

A Tons — and they change all the time. But to paraphrase a favorite one from Charlie Munger, any year you don't change your mind on something important to you is a wasted year. Right now, one of my guideposts, said to be from Goethe, is: "Cease endlessly striving to do what you want, and learn to love what must be done." Another right now, which I first saw in my grandmother's kitchen:

"The hurrieder I go, the behinder I get." That is so hard to learn, especially when life is so hectic. Slow down!

Q What lesson have you learned over the years that has stuck with you?

A For me, sanity and success comes from reading and running. And nothing quite matters like how well I treat other people.

Q What illuminating, instructive, and/or inspirational thoughts can you share that reflect your perspective on that time in your life?

A To quote [G. K.] Chesterton, "I was engaged about that time in discovering, to my own extreme and lasting astonishment, that I was not an Atheist."

Q What advice would you tell your 21-year-old self, knowing what you know now?

A I try to see any regrets as present calls to action. For example, I came to wish I'd taken Latin in school, so a few years ago I signed up for a Latin course (I only made it about halfway through; it was astonishingly difficult). Any regrets that surface about the way I've treated people, like my family or coworkers, I've tried to make amends and change my behavior. I'm always thinking, What kind of person do I want to be? Am I living that out each day?

Q **What would you tell someone about to turn 21, based on your experience?**

A Stay true to your eight-year-old self. The one who dreams big and gets excited about the good stuff and hasn't gotten swept away by the culture yet.

" And nothing quite matters like how well I treat other people. "

Kelly Evans

Look at what you want to do rather than the position you want to have

Dr. Leana S. Wen

Baltimore City's Health Commissioner

When she became Baltimore City's Health Commissioner in January 2015, **DR. LEANA S. WEN** had just turned 34. But then Wen is used to early breakthroughs: This physician and public-health advocate graduated from California State University at 18 — about ten years after she and her family had moved from Shanghai to California. Her career as a doctor, advocate and consultant has taken her all over the globe, but it's in Maryland that she has chosen to settle and try to make a difference. Typical of her open-minded and open-hearted approach is the title of her 2013 book, co-authored with Dr. Joshua Kosowsky: *When Doctors Don't Listen: How to Avoid Misdiagnoses and Unnecessary Tests.*

Q When did you realize what you wanted to do with your life?

A I knew very early on what I wanted to do but I didn't know how to get there. I'm an immigrant — my parents and I sought political asylum in America when I was eight. We came from China with less than $40 to our name and we struggled for many years to get by. My parents were professional in China and ended up cleaning dishes, working as housekeepers in hotels and doing menial jobs — working many jobs, in fact, for our family to stay afloat. I saw the many issues that come with poverty, including what happens when people die from preventable disease. In Los Angeles, I had a neighbor, a young boy, who had severe asthma. I was probably 11 and he was eight when he started having an asthma attack and wheezing. We gave him an inhaler but he was getting worse and worse, to the point that he couldn't breath at all. My instinct was to call 911 but the family was illegal and didn't want to call 911 for fear that they would be deported. That left an indelible mark on me. I still remember all the sounds and the fear and the anger that I felt. I had anger towards the family: How could they do this to their own child? But I had so much more anger for a system that would put people in positions like this, where we're choosing not to save people's lives because of their ability to pay or their immigration status, because of these unfounded reasons. At that moment I wanted to become a doctor: I wanted to prevent other children, other families, from suffering that same fate. The problem was that I had no idea how to actually do it: Nobody in my family was a doctor, nobody that I knew was a doctor. Maybe I went to a pediatrician for my asthma but otherwise I didn't know any doctors. The battle for me wasn't what I wanted to do, but how to get there.

Q Did you start orienting yourself toward science in high school?

A I didn't go to high school. I started college when I was 13. My family was in a difficult situation financially and with our immigration status. I needed a way to stay in the country, to have money and also to keep with my education. There happened to be a program at California State University in Los Angeles that I could enter. I tested into it when I was 13 and started college while also working in a laboratory as a tech. It was a work-study program that enabled me to continue my education and as a result I graduated college and entered medical school at Washington University in St. Louis when I was 18.

Q Why did you also pursue degrees in Chinese history and history?

A It was after medical school. I won the Rhodes scholarship and became a scholar at the University of Oxford.

Q Was that part of an effort to broaden your horizons before starting work as a doctor?

A It wasn't until after I entered medical school that I saw the failure of our medical system. I thought I could help this child with asthma survive, for example, but then I would see other children with asthma come in and I could give them inhalers or steroids, but it didn't change the conditions in which they lived. I couldn't change their homes and the allergens they were exposed to. I couldn't change these other things that actually determined how they lived. So it's those other things I wanted to gain understanding of and experience in. I took one year off medical school to become the president of the American Medical Student Association, which is a national advocacy organization for healthcare reform, and I worked on healthcare-access issues in Washington, D.C., and lobbied on behalf of patients for a year. That was instrumental in helping me understand that physicians have a larger role to play in society, not only in treating patients on an individual level but also in advocating for them and doing what is right. In St. Louis I also worked as a community organizer on issues like reproductive health and access to choice. All those issues helped me see that I needed to get further training in economics and policy. That's why I went to Oxford at the end of medical school. That experience was necessary for the work I do now, at the intersection of medicine and politics here in Baltimore City.

Q Was there a specific moment when you realized you could treat one person but you were not treating the environment that made that person sick?

A A young boy always came to the E.R. because he needed treatment for his asthma. I knew what to do for his asthma but I also found out that he and his mom were homeless and they were going to shelters where everybody smoked. When they finally found a place to live, it was a row house with two houses next to it that were vacant and full of allergens and mold. No matter what we did for that child in the hospital, he was always going back to an environment that was making him sick. In Baltimore, depending on where a child is born, that child can expect to live 65 years or 85 years, and we have to think about how just is a society where someone's zip code completely determines the outcome of their life and even whether they live.

Q **What did turning 21 mean to you?**

A I don't think I was in a very different spot from most
21-year-olds: I was searching. I think that a lot of 21-year-
olds are looking for how to make a difference. I'm struck
by the number of millennials who genuinely want to do
the right thing and are looking for the best way to do
that. For me at the time, it was, first of all, being willing
to find something else. It's hard to stop what you're doing
and find something else. It was hard for me to leave a path
that actually was what I wanted to do — I wanted to be a
doctor, it was my dream. So to leave medical school and try
community organizing and policy work was hard because
it was not what I initially thought I would do. But it was
important to have that experience. That's part of it: to
jump into something. I would highly recommend that to a
student. You don't know what you like doing and how you
can be impactful unless you try. The other thing I did at
the time and I would highly advise students is: don't wait.
I hear a lot of young people talk about how they have this
dream and they want to wait for that perfect opportunity.
Maybe they want to work on HIV in sub-Saharan Africa,
which is great, but they end up waiting until they have the
ability to do that. I would happily advise that student not to
take that route: They should get involved wherever it is that
they are, instead of waiting for that perfect opportunity.

Q **In your case, your questioning led to public health. Do you still have a practice?**

A I still practice emergency medicine. My path here wasn't straightforward, and nor should it be. For people who want to make an impact, there is no "you do this first and then you do that." The most important thing is to look at what it is that you want to do, instead of what position you would want to have.

"My path here wasn't straightforward, and nor should it be. "

Dr. Leana S. Wen

Do what you're passionate about

Benj Pasek & Justin Paul

Academy® & Tony® Award Winning Composers

BENJ PASEK and **JUSTIN PAUL** had quite the year: In 2017, they won the Oscar for Best Original Song for *La La Land*'s "City of Stars"; a few months later, they won the Tony for Best Original Score for the Broadway hit *Dear Evan Hansen*. The pair also contributed a song, "Runnin' Home to You," to a musical episode of the CW series *The Flash*, and have been writing numbers for the Hugh Jackman movie musical *The Greatest Showman*.

And they're just 32.

But then they got an early start: Pasek and Paul wrote their first show, *Edges*, when they were sophomores at the University of Michigan. The two collaborators went on to increasing success in the musical-theater world with shows such as *Dogfight*, *A Christmas Story, The Musical* and, of course, *Dear Evan Hansen*, in which an anxiety-ridden high school student finds himself embroiled in an escalation of lies. With their melodic tunes also heard in movies and on TV, there really is no stopping Pasek and Paul.

Q Tell me about your mindset when you were in your late
A teens?

Justin Paul: I grew up in Westport, Connecticut, and I
was lucky to go to a high school that very much valued the
arts. I was in jazz band and symphonic band and orchestra
and choir and a cappella choir. I played in school musicals
then I got to conduct them. I had pipe dreams of going
to music school but I didn't think it was possible for me.
In my junior year I was looking at colleges and wondering
where would be a nice, warm place to go to college, and
then go on to law school from there. The summer before
my senior year, I was in a musical and someone came up
to me afterwards and said, "I hope you're going to study
musical theater in college, that you'll keep going." The
thought had not occurred to me that I could do that. I
started looking into music schools and identified some
schools that had a really good musical-theater program. I
auditioned at the University of Michigan and got in.

Benj Pasek: I grew up outside Philadelphia and went to a
Quaker high school, which is common to the area. I had
a teacher in our 6th grade chorus, we did "A Weekend in

the Country" [from Stephen Sondheim's *A Little Night Music*]. Not your standard fare. I had teachers who really wanted to push the envelope, and I was very lucky to be in an environment that allowed that to be the case. My mom [Kathy Hirsh-Pasek] is a developmental psychologist and she would write a lot of children's music when we were kids. She and her collaborator [Mona Goldman-Zakheim] did five albums of children's songs. So I grew up watching my mom translate life moments into song form, taking an idea and distilling it to two or three minutes. That was something I was always interested in. Around 11 or 12, I was writing crude pop songs. That became something I sort of used as little diary entries, ways to recount moments in my life.

By the time I was in high school, I did this thing called the Philadelphia Songwriters Project, where I would go and do songwriting activities, meet other young songwriters.

I definitely thought about pursuing a liberal-arts education and did apply to schools for musical theater and to regular academic universities. I'd attended Carnegie-Mellon pre-college and Michigan was a place everybody talked about, they had amazing alumni. I applied early and I think I found out in late November/early December of my senior year.

Q You met very early on at Michigan, right?

A JP: We met at freshman orientation actually. Our particular group that we toured the university with had only two or three musical-theater majors. We became best friends even before school started. We bonded because we were terrible ballet dancers and hid behind each other in ballet class — we were performance majors so we had to take all kinds of dance classes, obviously acting and singing and all of that.

Q Did you have mentors?

A BP: We definitely had professors who were instrumental in helping us. Our sophomore year we were cast in terrible roles in a production of *City of Angels,* so we decided to write our own show, which ended up being *Edges.* We made our moms proud and all that. Once we had written that show, we thought maybe we could write more songs. In terms of craft, early on we were in performance classes and we were learning what actors need to make songs "actable": What does the character want? What are the obstacles getting in the way? How does a song keep moving forward? Learning those requirements for theater songs for actors, we just thought, "Well, let's just reverse-engineer this and put this into the songs we're writing."

Once we began to pursue songwriting a bit more seriously, the teachers began to design programs for us to help us learn more. The head of the program, Brent Wagner, would take songs by classic composers — but trunk songs that you might not know — and had me write lyrics to preexisting music, then compare our instinct to theirs.

JP: I did an independent study working with one of the teachers on cabaret arrangements, reharmonizing things. They were all committed to helping us explore the path we were interested in.

Q **What happened after college?**

A BP: We graduated early. We'd already met people who were mentors to us, like Jeff Marx, who co-wrote *Avenue Q*, and David Zippel. We spent our summers in New York and met all these writers. And also Stephen Schwartz, in a big way. After college, we wanted to meet everybody and we thought *Edges* would get us jobs. You know, "You liked our song cycle at age 19, then you'll hire us for your next show!" We would have all these meetings with people and the feedback we got was, "It's great that you wrote this thing — what's next?" It was only when we ran against this wall that we realized we had to generate our own work. We were meeting with people who were young playwrights and whom we thought would be fun to write with. Justin had a friend from middle school and high school, Peter Duchan, who was a big theater buff and who gave us the DVD of *Dogfight* to watch. We really responded to the film and saw potential in adapting it for a musical. I guess that was the first project we started after school. We acquired the rights ourselves because nobody was pursuing that indie film to turn it into a musical, as opposed to trying to go after a big property. We knew if we were going to do this, we needed to write about something we felt passionate about, something we wanted to explore. As soon as we began to think that way, ironically other works began to come to us. But I think we had to be in a mindset wanting to write for ourselves and wanting to write stories we connected with. We were approached for *A Christmas Story* before *Dogfight* was produced. We were really writing them at about the same time. Also during that time we were also writing an adaptation of *James and the Giant Peach*, on which we worked with Graciela Daniele at Goodspeed. We were developing all of those shows between 2008 and 2011. So *Dogfight* was our New York debut. *A Christmas Story* debuted in Seattle then went on a national tour. We didn't really expect it to come to Broadway and it did. Having both of those shows in the same year was unexpected and amazing for us.

Q Looking back, is there anything you'd tell your 21-year-old self?

A JP: Damien Chazelle wrote a beautiful line in *La La Land*: "People love what other people are passionate about." I don't think we ever really thought that would be the case for us. *Dear Evan Hansen* is certainly not something we thought people would gravitate towards. We wrote it as something we wanted to write for ourselves. We don't chase something because we think it's something people will want to watch. There's so little ability to predict what will rise to the surface and what won't see the light of day. In terms of making art, it's impossible to predict what will be commercial or what won't be, what kind of audience something will find — it may find audiences you weren't expecting. If we're passionate about something, it will find an audience, the scale of that doesn't really matter. You can't predict anyway so you might as well follow what you're passionate about.

BP: You work harder when you're excited about something. If it feels like pulling teeth or that you're doing it as a job, you don't have that natural enthusiasm that will push your project forward. The only other thing I'd say was a big shift for us was, we were in college around the time FaceBook and YouTube started. We found some success with having our songs online and early on I think we focused a little bit too much on wanting to write songs that people could sing at auditions or songs that we could do concerts with. Ultimately we realized that songs are different from shows and the construction of a song in a show is very different from the construction of a song outside of a show. It's important to really take the time to work on something and not seek the validation of showcasing a song at [cabaret venues] 54 Below or Joe's Pub before it really goes through draft upon draft upon draft, to make the work as good as it can be. This is the case with many millennials: You want to put your work out there, be seen and be heard, and I think we sometimes did that too early, to our own detriment. I think that was a big shift for us. We did a concert in 2008 at the Zipper Factory and we felt empty after it. We realized we should be writing shows and taking the time to study instead of presenting our work.

> "You can't predict anyway so you might as well follow what you're passionate about."
>
> Justin Paul

Find something that gets you up in the morning and go do that for your career

David Freed

Netpower/Clean Energy Manager

At 29, **DAVID FREED** has figured out something it takes many people a lot longer to figure out: "We're not going to solve some of the world's big challenges with small ideas." While many tech-minded millennials are happy creating apps to improve restaurant delivery, for instance, Freed realizes our planet is facing more pressing issues. One of them is the creation of clean energy. So this entrepreneurial Californian turned North Carolinian joined and became a principal at 8 Rivers Capital, an investment firm specializing in ambitious, game-changing ideas. He is 8 Rivers' project manager for NET Power, a potentially ground-breaking company that would create energy but no atmospheric emissions. For Freed, tech, entrepreneurship and large scale go hand in hand.

Q **What set you off on your career path?**

A I think I was more excited about the entrepreneurial thing than I was specifically by energy. I didn't really know entrepreneurship was a thing in high school. I never really focused on that — I was more interested in nonprofits. I studied all the classes you can expect to do, all the AP classes. My degree in college is actually in biomedical engineering, which is very different from energy. I did that because I thought I wanted to be a doctor. I quickly got more excited by entrepreneurship than in becoming a physician and staying in school for a long time. I joined different clubs, I started little, fun businesses when I was in college at Duke as part of these groups: We put ads on the side of Solo cups and gave them away to students, selling the advertising to make a little extra money — we called that "Media Cups." As part of a senior design project, they hook you up with some physicians at Duke Hospital and you design a device to solve a problem they have. A buddy and I took our devices and formed a company around them, which had never been done before. I met one of the founders of 8 Rivers at an entrepreneurship week I was helping run. They ended up funding us.

Q Were you still in college?

A It was near the end of senior year. I already had a job at BCG, the Boston Consulting Group. I felt that was the more responsible thing to do, but I didn't do it for very long at all, under a year — I quickly realized I wanted to be closer to technology and entrepreneurialism, I wanted to be closer to being an operator, so I came back and worked on my company. My co-founder had just finished his Master's so we decided to work on our company. It didn't go as we'd hoped but it was a learning experience. We were focused on ophthalmic medical devices. We had one for cataract surgery and one for macular degeneration. In the case of the cataract one, the engineering was a lot harder and a lot more expensive than we thought. We also heard a competitor was coming in with a laser that was going to completely destroy our market and force us into the developing world, which some of our investors weren't interested in doing. The other device wasn't a big enough opportunity for us. So we decided to wind the company down. I started to help on the energy project — this was back in 2011. The more I learned about it, the more I realized the challenges were there. When I was in school, that was kind of the big bubble around tech, when John Doerr gave his famous speech where he cried for his daughter and said we have to invest in this to make the world a better place for our kids [a TED Talk from 2007]. It was a great speech, and I always knew it was a problem but had never really focused on it. We had this technology that seemed like a good concept so I got really into learning about energy. I didn't do the technical work at that time; mostly I supported a lot of the marketing and financial work, because I'd done that when I was in consulting. Now I split my time between commercial and technical things, which is fun, I enjoy that.

Q Can you tell me a bit about 8 Rivers? They were pretty small when you joined, right?

A I was employee No. 5 or so. Now we've crystallized the model around doing large, sustainable infrastructure and technology development. We focus on technologies that we think will have a billion-dollar impact and solve global problems. Energy is one, cheap space launch is another, and the third is high-speed wireless access to information. We've got a few other things in agriculture and transportation that we've been looking at. Over the years, we've refined the model. Originally we were more of a VC — venture capitalist — so we would invest in companies. It was all partner capital, we don't have a fund or anything. We played around with different concepts, web apps, things like that. We realized what we're really good at is large-scale innovation. For NET Power, which is where I spend most of my time, we've been working with CB&I, Exelon and Toshiba. So you've got a big engineering company, a big power company and a supplier. The four of us were the initial consortium and decided to go out and build this project. That was a lot of fun, learning how to pull together a four-party agreement.

Q **What's ground-breaking about NET Power?**

A Our goal is to create power that has no carbon emission, no emissions at all, at the same cost as other technologies that do emit. We focus on natural gas and capturing the carbon from natural gas using a technology we came up with that we call the Allam Cycle. Most power plants since forever have looked to boil water as effectively as possible to drive a turbine with steam. Originally it was coal, then it was nuclear, and then we developed jet engines and we called them gas turbines. But all of them were figuring out how to boil and use water as efficiently as possible to make steam. We've realized that steam is actually not the best thing you should use — you want to use carbon dioxide. The capturing of carbon dioxide becomes an afterthought because you're already circulating it in your system. You don't have to "capture" it, it's already captured; it's more a production of CO_2 than it is a capturing of CO_2. We've raised over $140 million in order to build a 50-megawatt plant in La Porte, Texas, which is southeast of Houston. We broke ground in 2016.

Q **You're young and working on game-changing projects.**

A I don't think it's as hard as people think. The scale scares people — you think maybe you should let other people who have more experience do that. Being in it, there's a lot that young people can bring to large-scale innovation. I believe we're not going to solve some of the world's big challenges with small ideas. We need people who are big thinkers and big executors. We should try and fail, and that's OK as long as you keep going, refining along the way. No one wants to fail but we should make big bets. My justification for leaving the secure world of consulting and the nice path it would have created was: I'm in my early twenties, I don't have a lot of responsibilities, I don't have kids, I don't have a wife, I don't need a huge amount of disposable income — so why not take the risk now to do something that could change the world? If it fails, I can always go back and get the normal job. This is a way for me to take my shot. There's no place that allows you to do that like entrepreneurship. A lot of people want the security of mentorship from a big company. I was a little bit more adventurous and wanted to do something different. Entrepreneurship is a daily rollercoaster and it's really hard emotionally to deal with that. So you surround yourself with people who can steady the ride. That's not for everybody but so far it's been really fun.

Q **Did you have a mentor or someone who was instrumental in the way you approach things?**

A I had lots of great teachers and professors in high school and college. Even now I have great mentors at 8 Rivers. I'm not shy about asking for support and help from people I look up to. I recently told some students that their .edu email address is the most powerful thing they have. When you or I send somebody an email, they think you're trying to sell something. As a student you're just trying to learn so you can reach out to whomever. When I was in school I reached out to several public CEOs and asked if they could come and talk to us. A lot of them ignored me but some said yes. When I was in college I needed money to go abroad so I sold ads in the back of a local directory, the Duke Directory. I got used to going to 35 businesses a day in Durham, Chapel Hill and Raleigh, and walking in and asking who I could sell advertising to. This was in 2008, when the economy was in the dumps and nobody was buying print advertising. I heard "no" way more than "yes" but it helped me a lot. With NET Power and 8 Rivers, we've heard "no" way more than we've heard "yes." And "no" comes in all different forms. I get it, otherwise it would be obvious and there would be a thousand people doing it.

Q Are you in a position now where people come to you for advice?

A Sometimes, and I try to pay it forward as best as I can. Students reach out to me. I almost never say "I don't have time." My advice is always, find something that gets you up in the morning, that gets you excited, and go do that for your career. Don't do what you're supposed to, what your parents think you should, because eventually you'll resent that and you won't do as good a job. If you're excited about it, no matter what it is, go do it for a little bit, figure out if you can make some money at it — chances are you'll be creative and you'll figure out how to do that.

Q What would you say to your 21-year-old self?

A I was a junior in college then. There's a lot of specific things I would change but I'm pretty pleased with the general direction. I would say that it is okay to follow your passion. You hear that all the time as a young person, but most people ignore it. Once you get out of college, it's also really easy to fall into not eating right, not sleeping right, not working out. And not reading as much. I kinda fell out of that and got back into it in recent years, and that's made me a lot happier and healthier.

"Entrepreneurship is a daily roller-coaster and it's really hard emotionally to deal with that. So you surround yourself with people who can steady the ride. That's not for everybody but so far it's been really fun."

David Freed

Always be a kind and compassionate person

George Li

Concert Pianist

Piano prodigies often emerge at a very young age, and **GEORGE LI** is no different. Born in a Chinese family in Boston, Massachusetts, he was just four when he started learning to play the piano; five years later, he was making his orchestral debut with the Xiamen Philharmonic, and at 11 he was playing at Carnegie Hall. Li has won more competitions and prizes than we can list, including a silver medal at the 2015 International Tchaikovsky Competition, appeared with numerous orchestras, and performed in front of audiences worldwide — all the while continuing his studies, including a joint degree from Harvard and the New England Conservatory. Li's playing has been described as combining "youthful abandon with utter command" by the *New York Times*. And he still finds the time to follow sports!

Q Who or what influenced you in your teens/early adulthood?

A I have been always fortunate to have amazing teachers to guide and teach me all these years: Dorothy Shi, Yin Chengzong, Wha Kyung Byun and Russell Sherman. All of them have been imperative in helping me be the person, pianist and musician I am today, and I definitely wouldn't be here without them. I also remember being really inspired by pianists — Evgeny Kissin, Vladimir Horowitz, Martha Argerich, to name a few — when I went to hear them play in recital, or listened to their CDs. Later in my teenage years, I became influenced by great orchestras and conductors, as listening to such great artists helped inspire me to craft my own art.

Q Did you have a role model growing up?

A I've had several; I was very much affected and influenced by Vladimir Horowitz, for his daring creativity whenever he performed, as well as his limitless dynamic range and color palette. The conductor Carlos Kleiber was also a big role model, as his effortless grace and fluidity when guiding the orchestra through a symphony of Beethoven, for example, was a masterclass in itself. From a sports perspective (I'm also a sports fanatic) I always looked to Tom Brady and David Ortiz for their leadership and their will to win, no matter how dire the situation was.

Q **Was there a big challenge or big break in your teens/ early adulthood that led you to where you are today?**

A I'm not sure if there was one big break that led to where I am today, as I think that all the experiences that I've gone through have helped bring me here. But, I do remember one thing in particular that directly led to another once-in-a-lifetime event. In 2010, I had just won the Cooper International Piano Competition in Oberlin, Ohio. Almost one year later, I was invited to play at the White House for the German State Dinner! Turns out that the press secretary of the White House had connections with the Oberlin College, and asked the dean if he would recommend anyone to play at their event. Since I had just won the competition the previous year, he mentioned my name, and just like that, I was fortunate enough to experience something that I could only dream of.

Q **What motivated you to get to where you are now? What drives you every day?**

A I think my motivation has evolved over the years. Before, I thought of music as merely a hobby, and every day I was seeking to always better myself, be it technically or overcoming another challenge, etc. But then I realized through experience — both as a listener and a performer — how powerful music really was. This realization, coupled with the fact that there is an endless amount of repertoire that has been written for the piano, have driven me to keep practicing and striving every day.

Q **Could you picture what you would end up doing, or not at all?**

A I definitely didn't think I would get to where I am today, but since I was 10 or 11, I've always wanted to share the way I think and feel about music with as many people as possible; as long as I am still doing that, I'm pretty happy!

Q **When did you first realize you were into/good at what you do now?**

A I think I was 11 when I first realized how powerful music was. I was playing a concerto with a local community orchestra, and for some reason, I felt different when I was playing that day; I was completely taken away with the music, and the experience felt otherworldly. After the performance, people came up to me saying how much the music affected them, and for some it even changed their lives. I was completely taken aback by this, and from that day on, I felt that it was my mission to continue to craft whatever treasure I had uncovered.

Q Were your family and/or friends encouraging?

A Definitely; again, without them, I wouldn't be here today. For me, there was always "a village" of people who support and are always there for me, especially my family. With all the successes I've had, there naturally have also been many obstacles and hard times that I've had to overcome, and it was in those dark moments where my family was always there to support me, and to pick me back up on my feet, gently nudging me back in the right direction.

Q What was your school training like? Any particular memories of the conservatory?

A For high school, I went to an arts school called Walnut Hill School for the Arts, and they really helped give me time and space to work on music and piano, while also providing academic nourishment at the same time. It was much more flexible than public school, which was ideal for me since I had to practice and perform quite a bit during those years. I have fond memories of my time there, and I made so many great friends, many of whom I'm still in touch with.

Q **You've performed in front of heads of state? Is that particularly stressful or do you approach it like any audience?**

A For me, it was one of those moments and days that you want to cling to and make last forever, but in reality it just comes and goes in the snap of a finger. It was such an awe-inspiring moment for me, and I think I was really nervous when I stood in line to talk to President Obama and Chancellor Merkel, but as soon as I sat down to play, all the nerves ceased to exist, and it was only the piano and music that mattered.

Q **Do you have a favorite quote or mantra that keeps you going?**

A "Empty your mind, be formless, shapeless — like water." Bruce Lee

Q **What lesson have you learned that has stuck with you?**

A There have been many, but I think the biggest one for me is to always be a kind and compassionate person; as my teacher Russell Sherman said, "the highest of human qualities are charity and compassion."

Q **Did turning 21 feel like a big moment for you?**

A Actually, not really! I vaguely remember that day that I was allowed to drink, even though I ultimately didn't. There was a sense that I was officially a grown up adult, but I didn't really feel that different from the day before. It was a great day though!

"With all the successes I've had, there naturally have also been many obstacles and hard times that I've had to overcome, and it was in those dark moments where my family was always there to support me, and to pick me back up on my feet, gently nudging me back in the right direction."

George Li

10

Follow any crazy ideas, dreams and goals

Olivier Noel

Founder, DNAsimple

Just 28, **OLIVIER NOEL** is a busy scientist. While he's getting his MD/PhD at Penn State's College of Medicine, he's also exploring genetics in bariatric surgery at the Lewis Katz School of Medicine at Temple University. As if this weren't enough, he founded the company DNAsimple, of which he is CEO and which helps accelerate genetic research by connecting DNA donors with research scientists. After growing up in Haiti, Noel moved to New York City and attended Queens College. His goal is to connect the dots between medicine, science and entrepreneurship. In his spare time, he coaches a U16 team at the Fairmount Soccer Club in Philadelphia.

Q Did you have a role model growing up?

A Growing up in Haiti, I did not have many role models. In fact, I can think of only one person who I've looked up to as someone I wanted to be like and a role model. He was my neighbor and his name is Abdou Fall. He is a successful engineer from Senegal who had trained in Belgium and France before moving to Haiti following his marriage to a Haitian woman. He was different from anyone I had known or met at the time. He was extremely hardworking and professional, a great father, someone with a big heart, very cultured, always well dressed and loved by all. I was 12 years old when we became neighbors and friends, and at the time Abdou was the perfect person I wanted to emulate when I grew up. I wanted to be as well-rounded as him, and work as hard to be as successful.

Q Who or what influenced you in your teens/early adulthood?

A When I was about 14 years old, my father moved out and left us, my mother, my brother and I. I was angry, scared and felt like I had to instantly grow up and fill the void he had left and become the "man" in the house. At that moment, I pledged to myself to do anything possible — to go as hard as I can in school and in life — to not only help me take care of the family but would quietly prove to my father and others that I could still make it despite him deciding to leave. That turn of events was certainly one the most influential ones, if not the most, in my teens.

Q **What illuminating, instructive and/or inspirational thoughts can you share that reflect your perspective on that time of your life?**

A For me, giving up in the face of obstacles and difficulties was not an option. And that was pretty much my mindset since these early days. No matter how hard things get, no matter how helpless and lost I felt at times, I knew I would keep pushing until I found a solution. I always thought to myself that in every unfortunate or tough situation, there was always the option for it to get worse. And so, one can always find a positive in any situation, which can be turned into motivation to work hard and keep at something until a goal, or a dream is reached.

Q **What was your biggest challenge or biggest break in your teens/early adulthood that led you to where you are today?**

A My biggest challenge in my early adulthood was finding a way to pay for college and support myself after moving to New York from Haiti. At some point, I worked a combined five jobs to be able to make ends meet and get through school. At the time I was an international student and was not eligible for any loans or financial aids, and had to pay tuition out of pocket. Overcoming this challenge certainly played a huge role in making me the person I am today.

Q What were your dreams in your late teens/early twenties?

A I've loved science for as long as I can remember. I recall my very first chemistry class and simple decantation experiment we did in high school in Haiti, and I've wanted to be a chemist ever since. In college, I enjoyed my time volunteering in a hospital as much as I enjoyed doing research and running experiments in a lab. The idea of bringing new knowledge to the world through research and being able to apply that knowledge through medicine to positively impact lives is fascinating to me, hence I wanted to do both careers, and become a physician scientist.

Q Could you picture what you would end up doing, or not at all?

A Yes, a physician scientist. As far as becoming an entrepreneur, I always thought I would become one although I wasn't exactly sure when I would get involved with entrepreneurship considering that my MD/PhD training would take a long time. I'm glad it happened during my training rather than after.

Q **When did you first realize you were good at what you do now?**

A I've always been really good at math and the sciences in general in middle school and high school so I knew that I would end up doing something related to the sciences as a career. Although I was not 100 percent sure which one it would be. I did also realize that I could be a good entrepreneur in high school, when I used to make and sell CDs along with the lyrics to songs. This was the days when having a CD writer was a huge deal, and so I took advantage of it to make a few bucks.

Q **Were your family and/or friends encouraging?**

A They were there if I needed them. Although I am a very social person, I'm still not a big fan of seeking family or friends' support (moral or whatever), and naturally prefer to handle my affairs on my own. But I feel like people were generally encouraging when I did share my endeavors with them.

Q Do you remember your 21st birthday? Was it a big deal or just like any birthday?

A Not really, and not because of the alcohol. It was just like any other birthday honestly.

Q Do you have a favorite quote or mantra that keeps you going?

A I have two of them actually. "Live as if you were to die tomorrow and learn as if you were to live forever" and "The main thing is to keep the main thing the main thing" have been my favorite quotes/mantra for as long as I can remember. The last one is actually printed on a wall in my room and so I am reminded of it daily, just in case.

Q What lesson have you learned over the years that has stuck with you?

A There are a lot but I think one significant one is to not listen to the naysayers and simply follow the crowd. People are generally afraid to try to do the things that have never been done before or just things that they are not familiar with or comfortable doing. I've learned to question everything, go against the routine and what is "safe" and to follow any crazy ideas, dreams and goals that I feel that I want to accomplish. It sounds a bit cliché but it is literally the way that I live my life and something that has stuck with me over the years.

Q **What advice would you tell your 21-year-old self, knowing what you know now?**

A There's frankly not a whole lot that I would change if I could go back in time and so I can't think of life-changing advice that I would tell my 21-year-old self. I would probably recommend my younger self (it's "only" seven years ago that I was 21) to value family time a bit more and to actually try to create more opportunities to enjoy family members' company.

"And so, one can always find a positive in any situation, which can be turned into motivation to work hard and keep at something until a goal, or a dream is reached."

Olivier Noel

11

Stay hungry and stay humble

Brian Dumoulin

NHL Stanley Cup Winner

Few 25-year-olds can say they've won the Stanley Cup; even fewer can say they've won it twice in a row. Considering the way the Pittsburgh Penguins have been playing, their defenseman **BRIAN DUMOULIN** could have more accolades in his future. Born in Biddeford, Maine, Dumoulin won two NCAA championships with Boston College and was drafted by the Carolina Hurricanes in the spring of 2012, only to be traded to Pittsburgh. After spending some time with the Penguins' AHL affiliate, Wilkes-Barre/Scranton, Dumoulin joined Pittsburgh's roster full-time in the 2015-16 season. The rookie helped the Penguins win the Stanley Cup in 2016, becoming the first Maine native to hold that trophy. The following season, Dumoulin didn't let a broken jaw slow him down: He was back on the ice to help the Penguins win the Stanley Cup again.

Q Did you have a role model growing up?

A My role models growing up were obviously hockey players, but looking back at it now, it is easy to say that my role models were my parents. You always hear about the drives to and from hockey games and the costs of raising a hockey player. Hockey families travel thousands of miles and spend thousands of dollars just for the opportunity to play. Looking back I still can't get over the sacrifices they made for me: Every weekend was spent on the road and I can remember playing travel hockey in New Hampshire, where each game was at least an hour away. They sat there and watched every minute. Most of the time it was probably like watching paint dry but they always did it. Hockey parents are very unique and they definitely sacrifice the most of any sport. I talk to my dad now and I still think he misses those long drives. Fortunately, Pittsburgh is close enough that he can still make the drive down and catch a game every so often.

Q **What illuminating, instructive and/or inspirational thoughts reflect your perspective on that time of your life?**

A I just loved playing sports and competing. I think a lot of it was because I became best friends with my teammates. It wasn't just hockey, it was baseball, football, and other sports that helped me create friendships. I think my biggest takeaway from looking back at those years is to play every sport you can. I know it was tough on my parents, because they were always on the go, but it helped me makes friendships and develop relationships that I still have today.

Q **What was your biggest challenge or biggest break in early adulthood that led you to where you are today?**

A I think one of my biggest challenges in hockey was having people tell me what I should be doing. Coaches and teams were advising me to play for a prep school or specific junior hockey programs if I wanted to give myself the best chance to be successful. Pretty much everyone was telling me that I had to leave Maine if I wanted to play college hockey or be seen by scouts. Obviously, many of these guys had reached goals that I had set for myself, so I felt pressured to follow their advice. But I had a good core of people that told me, "If you're good enough, they will find you." I felt that as long as I continued to be challenged

and grow as a player, I wanted to continue to play in
Maine and New Hampshire.

Q Looking back, what motivated you?

A My motivation was really my love of the game. I really
loved everything about the sport of hockey growing
up. For as long as I can remember, I spent everyday
in the winter at the rink. Fortunately, throughout my
playing career I have had amazing coaches that have
instilled in me the passion for the game and the desire to
continuously improve. I was never the best on my team
when I was younger. I remember kids who were way better
than me and I still see them today and talk about those
old times. We always wonder why I became the best one
out of us and I really believe that I loved the game the
most and would do anything to go out there and play.

Q What were your dreams back then?

A My dream in my late teens was to play Division 1 college
hockey. Once I started being recruited and the goal began
to seem attainable, that dream turned into the desire to
play for the best team possible that would provide the best
academic opportunity possible. So I committed to Boston
College and soon after the dream continued to evolve. I
dreamed of winning a national championship, signing a

professional contract and most importantly graduating from Boston College. Graduating from BC has been the most important for me lately because I was offered a contract to leave BC after my sophomore year but I turned it down to go back to school. I knew it was very unlikely I would be able to graduate if I left after my sophomore year. So I went back and turned pro after my junior year, when I had eight classes remaining. At this moment I have only one class left. It has become tougher and tougher to go back each year, especially after playing into June. But I've remained committed to finishing what I started. I have three of the most challenging years of my life invested in working towards my degree and intend on making that effort worthwhile and graduating from Boston College.

Q Were your family and/or friends encouraging?

A In my teens most of my friends were hockey players and my parents' friends were all hockey players' parents. So everyone was very encouraging because we were going through the same process together. Hockey players and their families create bonds that last forever, regardless of where you come from.

Q What was school like?

A High school was amazing for me. I didn't want to leave

Biddeford High School. Plenty of people advised me to
leave but I had no desire to leave my friends or my school.
That's why I felt when I got the Stanley Cup last year
that BHS was going to be the first place I took it back
to. My senior year, when I ended up playing for the New
Hampshire Junior Monarchs, in Manchester, I commuted
after school every day driving an hour to practice and then
an hour back just so I could stay at Biddeford. I loved it
that much.

Q **What was going through your mind when you became
the first Maine-born NHL player to hoist the Stanley
Cup after the Penguins' victory over the San Jose
Sharks?**

A Lifting the Stanley Cup for the first time was the most
surreal experience of my life. It happens so fast and then
all of a sudden it was my turn to hoist the cup. There isn't
a specific order but usually it starts with the older guys
and then it is passed down the line. As I watched each
player hold it high, the anticipation of getting my chance
began to build. I would finally have my opportunity to
do what I dreamed about as a kid. Olli Määttä passed me
the cup and I lifted it up as high as I could. I only lifted it
for about 15 seconds, but it felt like forever. That's all the
time I needed, a quick skate, a twirl, and then hand it to
the next guy for him to enjoy.

Q **As a young player, how do you deal with competing in the NHL?**

A There is a lot of pressure playing in the NHL because obviously the fans expect you to win every night and I obviously want to win every night for them. Hockey is a game of mistakes and we aren't going to win every one, and I'm not going to play my best in every one. So there is a lot of pressure to make sure that the next game is my best one no matter what. We are fortunate to play the greatest game on Earth in front of incredibly passionate fans and we want to put our best effort night in and night out. The fans are not the only ones you feel the pressure to perform for: There are also your teammates, coaches, management, family and friends. That being said, hockey is a team sport and I try to focus on what I can control, and do my best every night to contribute whatever I can to the team's success.

Q **Do you remember your 21st birthday? Was it a big deal or just like any birthday?**

A For my 21st birthday I was in Wilkes-Barre, Pennsylvania It was my first pro season and the first time I had been away from my college roommates in three years. They were all going into their senior year at BC while I was in a foreign place meeting people for the first time. It was a tough year but I learned a lot and needed that step in my career to get to where I am now. It may not have been a typical 21st birthday, but it was a critical year in my life and my career as I transitioned from student to professional athlete.

Q **Do you have a favorite quote or mantra that keeps you going?**

A I've heard a lot of different quotes but my favorite one, and the one I remember the most, is, "Stay hungry, stay humble." My high school hockey coach, Jamie Gagnon, told me that back when I played for him. It's a very simple quote to remember and can be applied not just to hockey but to anything you do in life. It helps me remember to keep that hunger alive especially after finding success at a young age. "Staying humble" is even more critical because it reminds me of the importance of staying grounded, knowing where I came from and not being selfish or arrogant.

Q **What lesson have you learned that has stuck with you?**

A I don't know if this is a lesson or just something I have tried to develop over time, but I think it is important to have "thick skin." When you play the game on the stage that we do and in front to the passionate fans that we do, there will always be some that will be willing to share their thoughts on your play. Regardless of how hard I work, or how I play, there will always be those that will criticize or critique. I think it's important to hear what they have to say, good or bad, but not let it affect my approach. I have experienced it at every level of play, whether I was playing hockey in Maine, going through the draft process, in college, in the minor leagues and even now in the NHL after winning two Stanley Cups. My approach will always be to stay level headed and "stay hungry and humble."

---

66 . . . hockey is a team sport and I try to focus on what I can control, and do my best every night to contribute whatever I can to the team's success. 99

Brian Dumoulin

Design a life you'll love

Shane Gonzales

L.A. Fashion Designer

SHANE GONZALES started interning for Ruslan Karablin's iconic streetwear label, SSUR, just before graduating from high school. About two years later, the Canyon Lake, California, native was opening his own company, Midnight Studios. It was 2014, and Gonzales was 19. And things have kept moving fast. Fashion influencers like the rappers A$AP Rocky (who wore a Gonzales piece in the video for "Lord Pretty Flacko Jodye 2" in 2015) and Wiz Khalifa have sided with Midnight Studios, and the designer has created a limited-edition watch for the iconic Casio division G-SHOCK, whose mix of toughness, functionality and style make it a perfect match for Gonzales. Influenced in equal parts by "Tony Hawk's Pro Skater" video games and classic punk rock, Gonzales is still only 23. He's just getting started.

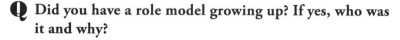

Q Did you have a role model growing up? If yes, who was it and why?

A Well, growing up I had several role models. My parents have always been at the top of that list, but other than that it was constantly changing due to the different interests I had over the years.

Q Who or what influenced you in your teens/early adulthood?

A Skateboarding, fashion, rock and roll, and hip-hop were what I was most influenced by back then as well as right now. People like John Lydon (Johnny Rotten) of the Sex Pistols, Japanese designers, Baker Skateboards, Public Enemy, etc. They all had major impacts on my life. The music I listened to and skateboarding were very much connected for me growing up. The music we skateboarded to would be in our favorite skate videos, it was everywhere skateboarding was. It had a message much stronger than anything else out there. It was very anti-everything, and mostly about standing up for what you believe in. As skateboarders we seemed to be the same way. We skateboarded when and where we wanted to and didn't quite care about anything else going on. Eventually that attitude and mentality led to what I wanted Midnight Studios to be. It took time to develop years later, but I feel it represents that same feeling skateboarding gave me, but through an artistic platform like fashion. The messages written on my clothes and the way I design all relate directly to my teenage years and young adulthood.

Q **What was your your biggest challenge or biggest break in your teens/early adulthood that led you to where you are today?**

A The biggest challenge at that point in my life was breaking out of the small town I was in and getting myself to a place where I could be free with whatever I chose to do and be recognized. Since I started doing what I do, it was difficult to progress and take it to the next step because of my age. I lived at home with my parents, I was in school, I didn't have money. It's hard to be taken seriously and move forward under conditions like that in the fashion industry.

Q **Looking back, what motivated you to get to where you are now?**

A I think at one point when I was in high school I just realized, "This is what I want to do. I'm going to be a designer." I would look at clothes and collections all day on the internet, at home, at school, anywhere. I started to understand that it wasn't that far of a reach for me. I would draw out designs on my homework as opposed to actually doing it, and researching everything required to start a label. I started making T-shirts and sweatshirts in my hometown but it wasn't quite what I was aiming for. I set myself a goal to move to Los Angeles once I graduated and start something completely new. In 2014, Midnight Studios was born in Los Angeles.

Q **What were your dreams in your late teens/early twenties?**

A I either wanted to be a professional skateboarder or a fashion designer. I just wanted to do something that involved having fun for a living and seeing the world. Those two met the requirements growing up.

Q **Could you picture what you would end up doing, or not at all?**

A Being a designer was a bit more clear for me after high school when I realized it was something I can potentially do for the rest of my life.

Q **When did you first realize you were into/good at what you do now?**

A The first time I really discovered fashion/streetwear was in middle school (6th grade) when I saw a Pharrell [Williams] or Kanye West video. The clothes they were wearing were different from what anyone else was wearing back then. I immediately thought to myself, "I want to wear and make clothes just like that." It took a bit of a different path, but that's what sparked my interest early on.

Q **Were your family and/or friends encouraging?**

A My parents helped me start my label back then. There was no way it would be where it is today without them. I had no money, no job, and needed help getting my ideas into the world. My whole family supported me, especially my brother.

Q **What was school like? A lot of people say high school or college was a turning point. Did you feel that way?**

A School for me was very interesting. It was all public schools and the town I came from had many different types of people and stereotypes. I think that contributed to me becoming a designer because I was so influenced by the everyday clothes kids were wearing, and I thought to myself that I could make clothes taking inspiration from all that I saw.

Q **Do you remember your 21st birthday? Was it a big deal or just like any birthday?**

A My 21st birthday wasn't a big deal. I just went out with a few friends that night. I think I made it up for when I turned 22.

Q Do you have a favorite quote or mantra that keeps you going?

A "Beauty is whatever anyone thinks is beautiful." Rei Kawakubo

Q What lesson have you learned over the years that has stuck with you?

A Patience. I used to rush things when I was younger because I couldn't wait and wanted something right then and there. That's not the way to go about things for me anymore. I have to wait it out and perfect something before I put it out to the world.

Q What advice would you tell your 21-year-old self, knowing what you know now?

A There's not much I'd change or tell myself. I'm quite happy with the way things are going. I'd say I was a bit more lost in what direction I wanted to take my brand and I feel like I'm figuring that out much more clearly now.

"I either wanted to be a professional skateboarder or a fashion designer. I just wanted to do something that involved having fun for a living and seeing the world. Those two met the requirements growing up."

Shane Gonzales

If it's not good,
take it off the table

Mike Wiley

James Beard® Award Winner

The James Beard Awards are to the food world what the Oscars are to movies: winning one is a major achievement. So it was quite a feat for **MIKE WILEY** and Andrew Taylor to win the Best Chef: Northeast category with their restaurant Eventide Oyster Co. in Portland, Maine. (This was their third nomination and first win.) In addition to the seafood-centric Eventide, Wiley, Taylor and manager Arlin Smith also own and operate the noodle-focused Honey Paw and the higher-end Hugo's.

Born in Portland and raised in Hanover, New Hampshire, Wiley, 36, took a winding road to professional cooking. After graduating from Colby College in 2003, this outdoor enthusiast moved to Colorado, where he ended up getting a Masters in rhetoric. But Wiley realized academia wasn't for him and ultimately chose the kitchen: Things happen for a reason.

Q **You didn't study cooking but English. Tell me about your mindset when you were in your late teens.**

A I was kind of a dork in high school: good student, active in theater. I wasn't really a big team-sports guy or anything like that. I spent a lot of time with my friends and family — I have a brother who's four years younger and actually works for me now, at the Honey Paw. My family was really big on academics. My father is since retired but he was an anesthesiologist; my mother's an English professor. So reading was always a big part of being a good kid in the Wiley house. I always thought that given my facility with schoolwork, I'd end up getting a doctorate and teaching. I went to Colby College, in Maine, and studied creative writing and literature and religious studies. I didn't have a practical bone in my body. I arrogantly thought that if something didn't interest me, why should I spend any time on it?

Q **Was food important in your family?**

A I had an amazing great-aunt who lived in Manhattan and we would go and visit her twice a year and it was always a very big deal for my father. He'd pick out a restaurant he was excited to eat at, we'd go out, have a nice meal. I think I associated restaurants with special occasions, celebratory venues. Anytime my brother or I got good report cards, we would pick a restaurant and our parents would take us to dinner there. My mother probably had a rolling menu of 13-15 different things that she'd cook. There wasn't tons of variety but she didn't have any time and it was pretty miraculous that she cooked us nutritious meals instead of serving us TV dinners or whatever. She had a copy of Betty Crocker's international cookbook and there was a recipe for pork-and-shrimp wontons. You'd make a simple meat farce with water chestnuts, scallions and little bit of cornstarch to thicken it, then you'd buy a whole bunch of dumpling skins and sit there and fold wontons for hours and hours. My mom would pay me something like a tenth of minimum wage — I was ten years old and had small fingers so I could bang out a whole lot of them. Then she'd freeze them in batches. She'd do that before Thanksgiving and the holiday season happened so she could just go to the freezer and pull out a couple of ziplock bags of them, fry them off or steam them off, and call that hors d'oeuvres for cocktail parties.

Q **Do you remember what things were like when you were 21?**

A I had graduated college and I was at home. I remember taking the LSAT and being not excited about spending the rest of my professional life with the people who were in that room. I was still in gut-reaction decision-making mode. It was just, "No, I'm not doing that" and I did not apply to law school. I know I wasn't up to anything particularly interesting, that's for darn sure. I just wanted to do what I liked until I found something I really loved and felt like it clicked.

Q **What did you learn when you started cooking professionally?**

A I got into cooking because in college I fell in love with rock climbing. As a skinny, flexible guy it offered a trajectory of improvement and understanding that had eluded me when I tried playing baseball or lacrosse. I fell in love with that and all my travel opportunities revolved around alpine skiing or rock climbing. Not surprisingly after graduating from college [in 2003] I moved out west to Colorado to pursue that. That's really when I started cooking professionally. I worked at a place called Le Bosquet, in Crested Butte. There wasn't a great mind behind the food, it was more of a collective endeavor. It was great. That's where I grew to appreciate being a line cook in a fast-paced kitchen. One season, they hired a guy who had worked at Charlie Trotter's in Chicago. I remember once we had finished our prep list for the day and he was like, "Well, we're all done with everything, maybe we could make something and put a special on." I was like, "What's a special?" The owner was like, "Yeah, that's great, just don't waste a lot of money." So we made a little potato pavé with some kind of wild-mushroom ragù. I realized that you don't need to have a recipe, you can be a little creative. I started thinking about trying to be economical and responsible with product, and trying to bring as much use out of a thing as possible. That's when I really started reading cookbooks and taking more interest in the craft, not just speedy execution.

Q **How old were you around that time?**

A I was probably 25. That was before I went to grad school. I applied to the University of Colorado at Boulder and was barely accepted. I specialized in rhetoric. That proved to be kind of silly but it was useful in that I got a Master's and didn't have to pay for it, I got teaching experience. And I was able to walk away knowing that ultimately I didn't want to be in academia. I spent the whole time being in kitchens. I wrote my graduate thesis on the aesthetic rhetorics of the French Laundry cookbook [2009].

Q **When did you decide to move back east?**

A I left grad school having worked as an unpaid intern with chef Eric Skokan at the Black Cat in Boulder. We got along really well and I was happy to work for free three nights a week just to learn things. Ultimately he hired me as a cook and I became his sous-chef. But I'm a crusty New England guy at heart and everyone in Colorado was way too fit and way too friendly. I saw that Hugo's was looking for a fish cook and thought I could learn a lot there: What better place to be a fish cook than in Portland, Maine? I wrote a really pompous cover letter, auditioned for the job and was hired.

Q **What did your book-loving family think of your decision to be a professional cook?**

A They were incredibly supportive. My mom's fond of saying, "I'd rather you be dead than lazy." They knew I was working hard and that I really enjoyed what I was doing. A lot of parents say, "I just want you to be happy" but I think that's really true with my folks. But I also went to grad school, and in the darkest, most puritanical side of their brains, they know I paid my dues.

Q **Did you have any mentors?**

A In the culinary world definitely Eric Skokan and Rob

Evans. Rob was the owner of Hugo's along with his wife, Nancy Pugh. When I was in middle school, high school and a little bit in college, I worked for a gentleman named Richard Wallace who ran Omer and Bob's, a ski and bike shop in Hanover, New Hampshire. I learned a whole lot from him about owning and operating a business. I got a sense of what it meant to be a member of a community, how important integrity and generosity was.

Q **How did you end up owning your first restaurant?**

A Rob [Evans] had been looking to sell Hugo's for a little while. Running a fine-dining restaurant is loads of work and it can feel like a battle sometimes. He had won the James Beard Award and had been in business for ten years, which for an independently owned restaurant is no small achievement. He heard I had a degree in writing and asked for help punching up the notice of sale for the business. I was like, "So much for job security." As it turned out, he had been telling Andrew that he should think about buying Hugo's. That conversation turned to me and how we should buy the place because there was a spot next door that we could turn into a more casual restaurant — that was the genesis of Eventide.

Q **Portland is a great city for food. Do you feel it's important to be part of a community?**

A Oh yes. There's the restaurant history in Portland and Maine, and then there's the agricultural and fishing history of Maine — the latter two being really old. Maine has been providing lobsters, potatoes and apples to the rest of the country for hundreds of years and hopefully will continue to do so. The depth of farming skill and knowledge, and likewise for fishing obviously, is jaw-dropping here. No place else I've cooked has markets as abundant as they are here. I feel like a lot of what we're able to do with food comes because there's MOFGA (Maine Organic Farmers and Gardeners Association), an amazing group that puts on the Common Ground Country Fair every year where farmers get together and share techniques and ideas. Maine is one of the oldest states in the nation. Not for its founding dates but its demographics: We have a lot of old people, and a lot of them are farmers. There's a big push in the agriculture community to preserve that land and make sure the future is secure, but also pass down the knowledge of how to grow things successfully and responsibly. And not only do we have great raw products to work with and a great community, but our dining public is great. And because they're crusty New Englanders, if they think you're serving something that's bullshit, they will let you know. That's important.

Q **Knowing what you know now, what would you tell your 21-year-old self?**

A Things are pretty mercurial. I don't know that I was meant to cook. Maybe if I'd gone to a different grad school, I would have enjoyed my program more and continued on. The difference between being somebody who's a happy and successful cobbler and somebody who's a happy and successful professor — it's not too different, I think. If I talked to my 21-year-old self, I would say, "Stay busy, keep doing challenging things, work really hard and try to make sure you're doing things that you like." Whenever I made a decision like, "I know I don't want to do this, that's not good," it narrowed the field for myself: That's off the table, I know I don't want to do that. That allowed me to say, "OK, maybe I'll take another look at cooking. Maybe that's the thing I'm supposed to end up doing."

"I got a sense of what it meant to be a member of a community, how important integrity and generosity was."

Mike Wiley

14

Take the drama out
of your finances

Stefanie O'Connell

Finance Blogger

STEFANIE O'CONNELL has made her name providing financial advice to millennials, but people of all ages would be well-advised to follow her common-sense approach. O'Connell, 30, did not go to business school or work at an investment fund: Her experience comes from having to live on very little money when she was out of college. Being an actress was her passion but she wasn't earning much, so O'Connell made up for her relatively low bank balance with a high level of personal discipline. In her 2015 book *The Broke and Beautiful Life: Small Town Budget, Big City Dreams*, inspired by her blog of the same name, O'Connell laid down the basics of financial literacy and shared some of the tips that can help anyone live their dream — without going bankrupt.

Q Can you tell us a bit about your mindset in your late teens and early twenties?

A I was a competitive gymnast and I was also very involved in the drama department at school, in Connecticut. When it came time to apply to college I was dead set on going to an art school, but my parents said no, you still need to get a full-rounded education. So I did, and that's how I wound up going to NYU for a double major in drama and psychology. After graduating, I started working in theater full-time. It was a very sobering reality to, one, work in theater and two, work in theater in the middle of a recession — I graduated in 2008. I got a job in a show touring Asia and had a contract for a year, but about halfway through, in the fall of 2008, the producers canceled the rest of the tour and sent us all home. I wound up back in New York City in January 2009, an unemployed actress in the middle of a recession. It was a very big reality check in that moment. There were a lot of them over the course of the next four to five years, another being that the next job I was offered was for $225 a week, even though I was playing three main roles in three musicals. There were a lot of moments like that. I became more successful in the industry — for example I played one of the Whos in *How the Grinch Stole Christmas* at the Theater at Madison Square Garden — but the salary was $542 a week before taxes, agent fees and union dues, so I made $400 a week. And that's just not sustainable. As I got to be 26, 27, I was looking around, thinking, "This isn't it, this isn't the quote-unquote dream that I thought it would be." I realized that doing what I loved wasn't the same as having a lifestyle that I loved. Everything I was doing was requiring the sacrifice of literally everything else, not just financial stability but also being present in relationships, being able to go to a wedding. I was always not going to things because I had to be available for a show. In that industry somebody will always do your job for less — I felt very powerless and I didn't like that [*laughs*].

Q How did you get into money management?

A I felt out of control of my own destiny. I was somebody who was a high achiever and really strived in a structured environment, so I looked to money as a kind of grounding force: Numbers were a tangible part of my life and nothing else was. I wasn't making a lot of money but I could choose the way I was managing it, I could measure my progress — there was something really comforting in that to me.

So I started to learn more about it and as I did that, I noticed that people started asking for my opinion about things. I was taking concepts I'd been reading about in the jargon-filled books and newspapers, and I was translating it into an idiot's' guide. I was going through the process myself and sharing that experience: "Here's something we all have to deal with and a lot of us are intimidated by it, but we're all capable of. So here are my mistakes and my successes." I found there was a huge audience of people who were craving that kind of information presented in a really digestible format. Since I've had a book come out, I do speaking for a living, I help other people with money [matters]. It's been incredibly transformative. There's absolutely a huge shift in dynamics in terms of what's happening in terms of financial knowledge, financial access and financial community. You bring that to a new audience that's been discounted for a long time, and that's important.

Q **When do you think people should start thinking about money? In high school?**

A To be honest, I wish this conversation started immediately. You can teach a kindergartener the difference between saving, spending and sharing — that's the concept money management distills down to. But absolutely in high school. Going to college, the conversation is centered around prestige as opposed to return on investment or cost, which is a huge mistake. What happens is, that conversation [about money] doesn't really happen until after you're out and you have student loans that you can't pay off. I don't know why there's a system that lets a 17-year-old with zero credit history sign up for $200,000 of debt. There's no collateral other than their future earnings, and we don't even know that they're going to have good future earnings. It's kind of crazy that we're not having this dialogue from freshman year of high school, when people are starting to talk about why your grades are going to matter for college. Finance is largely a creative endeavor. For someone like me, who had a limited income for such a long time, it wasn't about giving things up but about finding creative new ways to do the things I wanted, but at a lesser cost. And that could apply for college as well.

Q How do you think parents can best help their children understand the stakes?

A It's important for kids to have skin in the game. If your child knows they're on the hook for their own discretionary spending from the time they become an income earner, whether that's from a summer job or a high school job or whatever, it's important for them to understand that there are expectations in place. And that's not just money to burn but money they need to buy essentials with, because that's the future. We're not teaching kids some of the most basic, practical life skills. The reason I don't think we do that is because, to be honest, most of our parents aren't great at managing money either, and they don't know how to have that dialogue. Kids do inherit their money habits, by and large, through observation.

Q **When did you realize you had a knack for money management?**

A When I was on tour with a show, I would get a per diem — an allowance to cover my hotel stays and my meals. I had started reading a lot of personal-finance literature while I was still acting and I would track literally everything I spent and earned in spreadsheets — I still do this. When I was on this one tour, my per diem was $54 a day, and it had to cover my hotel and my food. So I'd have to share a room at a really awful hotel, go to the grocery store. It was not fun. You don't pay taxes on your per diem, it's not like your regular salary, so I figured that if I spent less than this ridiculous amount of money each day, then I could save the rest for myself and it'd be tax-free. It wasn't easy but I would look at my spreadsheet and I'd have a column with $54 and I'd have the day's expenses, then subtract one from the other and see how much I had left over. I would get really creative. Anytime I went to a new city I would check FaceBook to see who I knew in that city to see if I could stay with them instead of going to a hotel. If I found somebody often they would give me food — they wanted to be a host. All of a sudden I wasn't the victim of how little money I made, I was the architect of how much money I kept. That was a huge mindset shift for me. People accept their bills, they accept their income, and they don't negotiate, they don't look for solutions.

Q Do you think there's a tendency to put your head in the sand when it comes to money?

A There is a lot of that. The basic money categories are spending, saving and sharing. Let's say a young child gets $10 for a birthday — that framework for their money journey gives them a solid sense that money doesn't all go into one place. If I have this $10 today, what does it afford me now and what does it afford me tomorrow, not necessarily one to the exclusion of the other but equal consideration for both, that's the goal. How do you fight against that YOLO [you only live once] mentality, how do you fight against the idea that you're just going to live for the moment? It's about making people grounded in the cost of their dreams. I do exercises with some of my followers. I ask them what they want in the next five years, to design their dream life. Once they do that, they have to break each item in that dream life into a number. If you have to save up $100,000 for a down payment for a house, that's $20,000 a year, not an insignificant amount of money. So we need to be thinking along the lines of, What are my goals and what are the actual costs of achieving them? And how does that break down into a yearly savings amount, a monthly savings amount — whatever makes it tangible for you. That's a good way to push against YOLO and procrastination. You also ask people, Are you okay not having that? Are you okay giving up those things?

Q **What if a young person says they want to follow their passion, which happens not to very lucrative?**

A I so understand this [*laughs*]. They need to consider what the financial reality of their passion is within the context of their other lifestyle priorities. When you say, "I'm going to follow my passion," you're talking about a career vertical and ignoring the rest of your life. And what tends to happen is that the passion eventually erodes away and you end up compromising every other lifestyle vertical. I'm not saying you shouldn't follow your passion, I'm not, but you need to make an investment with all of your values and priorities in mind, and not just one. The idea of creative problem-solving when it comes to finances is really transformative. This was a big thing for me: I wanted to tell the world I was financially stable and I also wanted to work on my own terms. Now I can do all of these things: I can make money anywhere in the world; if I walk into an audition, I can do so without the pressure of needing the money, which is a huge relief. I can walk away if the conditions or terms are unacceptable. For me, that power is so much more valuable

Q What would you tell someone who's turning 21?

A Part of it is a youth thing. The other part is, there are unique circumstances surrounding this generation. There is no longer a 40-year framework for your career where you have a college degree and you're set for life. But the interesting thing about millennials is that they were raised with that premise and then they flipped the script as they were in college or entering the workforce: You're learning in the moment. It's a much more practical approach because they already know that narrative is broken, whereas those who grew up with that narrative are now redefining everything.

Q Do you remember your own 21st birthday?

A I was working at a summer theater when I turned 21.

My birthday was on a day off, but we'd been scheduled to perform a few songs at one of the patrons' parties. We were welcome to the food and alcohol, which I took full advantage of, being 21. I didn't feel great at the end of the night, so I took some NyQuil. After falling asleep and waking up in the middle of the night, the combination of the alcohol and NyQuil had a horrible effect. I tried to go to the restroom but it was as if I had no center of gravity so I couldn't stand up straight and I kept bumping into things. I woke up the next morning with my lip split open and spent around eight hours waiting in the ER to get it stitched back up. I didn't have an understudy for the show so as soon as I got back from the hospital, I had to get ready to go on stage, lip stitches and all.

Q **Knowing what you know now, what would you tell your 21-year-old self?**

A Lessons learned: Don't take NyQuil after you've had a drink, and . . . the show must always go on.

> "I'm not saying you shouldn't follow your passion, I'm not, but you need to make an investment with all of your values and priorities in mind, and not just one."
>
> Stefanie O'Connell

Calm down and let go of
things you can't control

Brett Haley

Film Director

When people think of movie locales, they tend to think of New York or Hollywood, but **BRETT HALEY** made his first professional feature, *The New Year* (2010), in Pensacola, Florida. Haley had moved there when he was around nine, after growing up in Key West. Like many debuts, *The New Year*, which Haley co-wrote and directed when he was in his mid-twenties, had a low budget, but that only belied its creator's high ambitions. Now 34, the Brooklyn resident has added two well-received indie movies to his résumé: *I'll See You in My Dreams* (2015), starring Blythe Danner and Sam Elliott, and two years later *The Hero*, with Elliott this time starring alongside Laura Prepon.

Q **When did you decide you wanted to make movies?**

A I'd been making movies from when I was really little,
probably eight or nine. I made my first feature when I was
16 on what was called S-VHS. That's sort of how I bonded
with my group of friends — we would make these movies
around socializing. We'd be hanging out over the summer,
have fun, order pizza, watch movies and make movies. It
was part of my social life. In many ways I tried to get back
to directing because that's where I was most happy: I'm
truly most fulfilled when I'm on set. It's like I'm addicted
to that feeling of being on set.

Q **Did you know what being a director entails?**

A I think kids are really sophisticated now and they know
what a movie director is. When I was little, I didn't
understand that there was a job of movie director. I
loved movies but I looked at them more from the actor's
perspective: I was a fan of Bruce Willis or Jean-Claude
Van Damme — action movies. So to me it was sort of
like, "That's what I want to do: I want to be like Jean-
Claude Van Damme" because I loved the movies he was

in. I didn't realize there was a storyteller behind it, I could only see the actor. Eventually when I was around 13 or 14 I started seeing movies that I probably should not have been seeing, movies like *True Romance* and *Pulp Fiction* and *Goodfellas* and *Angel Heart* — darker movies that made me wonder, "Who comes up with this stuff?" Quentin Tarantino made me realize, "What that guy is doing is what I want to do." So when I realized that you could write and direct, that's what I started looking towards. I was obsessed and I haven't stopped since. It's really nice to know at a young age what it is you want to do with your life. It can also be maddening because the thing I want to do is not easy — it's hard [*laughs*]. It's been a challenge trying to build a career where I can support myself and my family. I think my parents were very worried about me for a long time [*laughs*].

Q Was there a mentor or an influential figure in your life?
A My brother [novelist Joshua Ferris] was a big influence on me growing up. We grew up in separate houses and he would send me mixtapes of Tom Waits and the Magnetic Fields. So when I was 12, I was listening to that kind of music. He was the one who showed me *True Romance*. We would talk about movies, we would talk about art. He made me read Raymond Carver short stories, Vladimir

Nabokov's *Lolita*. I'm a terrible reader, I have a difficult time staying focused on a book for a long period of time, but I did read. He was like, "You've got to watch *Twin Peaks*." Then later it was *The Wire*. We'd watch those together, talk about it. He was a big influence on what is good and what is not good. He was a tastemaker.

Q **You grew up loving action movies but that's not what you've been making as a director.**

A It would be an easier point of entry as a writer. But I always knew that if I wrote something that was too big or too good too early, then I would become a writer. The industry likes to put you in a box and if the first thing you come out with is a script that's too big, they're going to give it to somebody else. You then have to say to them, "Hold on, I'm actually a director." And they're like, "Yeah, yeah, we'll deal with that later." So my goal was always to make films that I could physically go out and make, for less money. I became obsessed with John Cassavetes after college. I read *Cassavetes on Cassavetes* and I realized that was where I needed to start: I needed to start with the basics, which were storytelling and performance. Then I made my first official feature film, *The New Year*, for $5,000 and with no crew, in Pensacola. I want to make what I can make; I don't want anybody to give me permission.

Q Did you go to film school?

A Yes, I went to the University of North Carolina School of the Arts. I made movies there, like a big fantasy kind of action movie. That's what I wanted to do. But then I realized that if I'm going to be a director, I needed to take a step back and write things that I could go and make. And I'm still sort of doing that. I think I'm on the cusp now of getting into more genre movies. What's great is that I think I've learned about characters and humanity and how important performance is, and all of those I can bring into the genre world.

Q Your last two movies star older actors, whereas young directors often go for stories about young people.

A Making *I'll See You in My Dreams* with Blythe Danner, I wanted to write a meditation about loss and about dealing with loss and dealing with grief, and how we get through that. The themes were important to me, and I thought, "If I'm going to write a film about grief and loss, I'm not going to write it about a bunch of 20- or 30-year-olds living in Brooklyn. That to me is not interesting." A 70-year-old widow seemed more interesting. I only thought of what was best for the story I was trying to tell. My co-writer and creative partner, Marc Basch, and I were really inspired by Sam [Elliott], and we just thought we'd write something else for him. I didn't think about it too much beyond that. I didn't care that he was of a certain age. I'm really from the gut in what I want to do. Right now I'm trying to make a film about a father and a daughter who start writing music together. It just came to me and I was like, "That's what I want to do." I don't know why. There are just themes I'm interested in, and let's go. So I try not to make my decisions too calculated.

Q **Do you have any memories about turning 21? Were you still in college for instance?**

A No, I turned 21 after college — I'm one of those young ones. My birthday is in August so I was on the cusp. I went to L.A. for a few months but it wasn't for me and I moved to New York. My brother was there, I had more friends there. I started working at a restaurant and living life, you know? Being in New York was really good for that. Eventually I was an assistant for a few directors, so that's how I got some experience.

Q **What did your family think of your career choice?**

A I think they're proud of me now, they're happy that I followed my passion. I think they were worried just because . . . I mean, a lot of filmmakers come from money, and that makes sense. There's no judgement against that:

When you have a safety net of money, it's a lot easier because you can have the time to write, the time to work. I've always had to hustle to get by financially, and I think my parents were a little bit worried [*laughs*]. I'm barely making a living now, and everybody looks at me and says, "Wow, you've done so well, you're such a success." The reality is that there's not a lot of money in independent film. I've had a lot of success and made more money than most have making independent films, but it's still difficult. I don't know if my parents were like, "Oh Brett was always going to make it" or if they're a little surprised. You'd have to ask them.

Q Looking back, what would you tell your 21-year-old self?

A I think I'm still trying to live out that advice: chill out. Everything happens for a reason. If things work out, they work out; if they don't, they don't. Things shake out in weird ways. I've yet to have the peak of success or the misery of total and utter disaster: I always end up somewhere in the middle, and I'm kind of OK with that. There's a lot of good that comes with it, and there's a lot of bad, and you just have to calm down and take these waves. Sometimes the surf will be really intense and sometimes it will be really calm. And you just go with it. And you just need to chill. The. Fuck. Out. Because you can't control it. I still need to take that advice. I'm a very passionate person and I'm very emotional and sensitive because I care so much. When things are not going my way — and this is not creative, it's all logistics: Is my movie going to get financed? Will it get into this film festival? Will it get bought? It's all the things I can't control. I love the creative so much because I can, to a large degree, control that. You have to be able to let go of the things you can't control. It's very hard to do that. I'd continue to scream that at my young self: just chill out, buddy.

---

66 There's a lot of good that comes with it, and there's a lot of bad, and you just have to calm down and take these waves. Sometimes the surf will be really intense and sometimes it will be really calm. And you just go with it. And you just need to chill. 99

Brett Haley

Teach yourself to cry
on the spot!

Eva Noblezada

Broadway Singer

Participating in the National High School Musical Theatre Awards (known as the Jimmy Awards) at the Minskoff Theatre in 2013 was a big deal for **EVA NOBLEZADA**. Not only was the Filipino-American student from North Carolina's Northwest School of the Arts singing on an actual Broadway stage, but she caught the eye of a judge who helped set up an audition with the mighty producer Cameron Mackintosh. The following year, Noblezada took on the lead role of Kim in the West End's revival of *Miss Saigon*. She was just 18. And things did not stop there: In 2017, Noblezada made her Broadway debut in the same part, celebrated her 21st birthday a few weeks later, and was nominated for a Tony. Nobleza did not win, but it still looks as if she has a bright future ahead of her and may one day join the most famous Kim, Lea Salonga, in the Broadway hall of fame.

Q Did you have a role model or mentor growing up?

A My role models were my parents, my auntie, Sutton Foster and any other performer or person I met who was kind-hearted, hard-working and beaming with confidence.

Q What influenced you in your late teens?

A I always loved fashion but never had the money so Salvation Army and Goodwill were my way of expressing my personality. I loved writing stories as well. I write today, too!

Q What illuminating, instructive and/or inspirational thoughts can you share that reflect your perspective?

A In my late teens, I was in London. I have snapshots of "Eva" throughout each stage of my life, each chapter. I had to soak up everything happening to me like a sponge. I had to learn quickly, all the while making sure I was never losing myself and forgetting who I really was. It wasn't perfect. I struggled a lot adapting to the independent lifestyle — let alone leading a West End musical and being in the spotlight.

Q What was your your biggest challenge or biggest break
A that led you to where you are today?

My big break was obviously the Jimmy Awards. But if I
didn't work my ass off in school I couldn't have brought
my A game. My parents instilled in me a really important
mentality of hard work and passion. They really go hand
in hand.

Q Looking back, what motivated you?

A My family motivated me. I wanted to do it for them. The
friends I made in London, who will forever be lifelong
friends, motivated me. And ultimately, my daydreams
motivated me.

Q Could you picture what you would end up doing, or
not at all?

A I could picture it. I would be the girl putting my head
outside the car window lip-syncing and imagining she was
in a music video. I was the girl hand writing every word to
my favorite films and studying each role no matter the sex.
I taught myself how to cry on the spot. I worked so hard.
And I always had that inkling in my gut that I would be
doing what I was in love with. But who could picture the
West End and Broadway without romanticizing it?!?

Q **When did you first realize you were into/good at what**
A **you do now?**

I was always singing since I was a little girl. I never saw it from the perspective of "I'm good." I always thought, "I'm pretty sure I told the story. I know I hit all the notes the way I wanted." During school, from 11 to around 16, I slowly grew my confidence.

Q **What was your 21st birthday like? Did you actually perform that day?**

A Yup. It's such a big deal [in the U.S.] but I really didn't care. I've been drinking for years.

Q **Do you have a favorite quote or mantra that keeps you going?**

A I have a few quotes — I don't only have one that I live by as I'm always changing. I love saying, "Never compare yourself to everyone else" and "Loving yourself is the strongest weapon you'll ever have." I have favorite books and audiobooks that help motivate me: *The Power of Vulnerability* by Brené Brown, *It Was Me All Along* by Andie Mitchell, *The Subtle Art of Not Giving a Fuck* by Mark Manson, *Women Who Run with the Wolves* by Clarissa Pinkola Estés. And to mix in with those I listen to a lot of history audiobooks or Greek mythology stories.

Q **What lesson have you learned over the years that has stuck with you?**

A Oh God, no way could I have learned just one lesson. I could write a book — and I'd really like to. I think overall through every struggle I've really learned to accept Eva as she is. And I couldn't go through life without that. I really love the "no-bs" filter I've strengthened. I think now it's just going with the waves of life. Enjoying and savoring each second, happy or maybe struggles.

" I had to soak up everything happening to me like a sponge. I had to learn quickly, all the while making sure I was never losing myself and forgetting who I really was. "

Eva Noblezada

Don't put stupid conditions
on happiness

Tony Tulathimutte

Award Winning Fiction Writer

TONY TULATHIMUTTE's first published story, "Scenes from the Life of the Only Girl in Water Shield, Alaska," appeared in the literary journal *Threepenny Review* and went on to win the prestigious O. Henry Prize in 2008. It was an auspicious beginning for the 25-year-old writer, but the reading public had to wait until 2016 for Tulathimutte's debut novel, *Private Citizens*. Set in San Francisco around 2007, the book tracks the experiences, including in the tech scene, of some recent graduates from Stanford — where Tulathimutte, who grew up in Western Massachusetts, got his B.A. and M.A., before attending the Iowa Writers' Workshop. *Private Citizens* was praised for his portrait of a specific time and place, hailed as one of the best books of the year by the likes of *The Guardian* and *The Atlantic*, and even landed Tulathimutte on *Late Night with Seth Meyers*. Now 34, Tulathimutte continues to mix up fiction and essays for publications such as *Travel + Leisure* and *The New Yorker*.

Q Did you have a role model or was there a particularly influential person in your life when you were growing up?

A I attended a weird, tiny private school in the Pioneer Valley that had been co-ed for like three minutes. I was goth until about tenth grade, when I made friends with precocious-arty-leftist-indie-rock nerds, in particular Liz, who was hyperarticulate and into sixties literature. We did projects at her place after school, like reenact *Iron Chef* or write song parodies for the school contest.

Q What was your your biggest challenge or biggest break that led to your becoming a writer?

A In college I took a fiction workshop on a whim with Adam Johnson, a hugely charismatic teacher who was good at selling the sizzle. The class did what writing classes are mainly supposed to do, which is get you excited about writing and aware of its possibilities (as opposed to making you a good writer, which comes many years later). The former CEO of Nike was also in that class for some reason.

Q Looking back, what motivated you to get to where you are now?

A At Stanford I had a group of friends who were exactly where I was at with fiction: excited novices with mostly skeptical Asian parents. We ended up forming a writing group and holding each other accountable, and we've all become writers — Jenny Zhang, Karan Mahajan, Alice Sola Kim, Anthony Ha, Vauhini Vara, Anna North, Esmé Wang. I know community gets ickily commodified in lots of ways, but a talented long-term writing group is the easiest way to get the feedback, encouragement, and deadlines you need to get through the rough early years.

Q What were your dreams in your late teens/early twenties?

A To be hipster scum, honestly, or at least be in a band. The only things I lacked were showmanship, talent, taste, artistic vision, attitude, motivation, and any desire to cooperate. Karaoke suits me better.

Q Could you picture what you would end up doing?

A Yeah, I'd be making a ton of money in Silicon Valley and then going home and extinguishing one lit match after another on my inner thigh.

Q When did you first realize you were into/good at what you do now?

A I won the undergrad fiction contest at Stanford, and the story went on to get published and win an O. Henry Prize. In retrospect I can see how giving young writers too much validation too early is actually paralyzing and makes them ravenous for all the wrong things — prestige, popularity, more awards. Felt great at the time though.

Q Were your family and/or friends encouraging?

A My parents absolutely, although I suspect it helped that I had high earning potential. My friends were my writing partners, so that was a given. The one discouraging me most was usually me.

Q Do you remember your 21st birthday? Was it a big deal or just like any birthday?

A By my 21st birthday I was still straight-edge. I didn't develop at all emotionally until I started drinking, smoking, and snorting things a while later, and even then it took a few more years before my self-awareness became useful for anything. I'm not saying drugs are good solutions to anything, but they do help unclench your ass, or clench it more interestingly. My big deal birthday was my 25th — I threw it at a weird eccentric mansion/commune in East Oakland called Mr. Floppy's Flophouse, a former bordello where Jack London used to hang out, and was founded by a guy who was searching for an inverted pyramid that he thought contained universal knowledge.

Q **What lesson have you learned over the years that has stuck with you?**

A I did an independent study with Elizabeth Tallent, and was six weeks past deadline on a story, the writing of which was basically a form of self-harm. I was 21, so everything I did seemed consequential. When I finally met with Professor Tallent, she listened to me squirm and make excuses for a while, and then she just said, "You know, Tony, nothing happens if you don't write." The double entendre was very cunning — she was either giving me permission to quit and stop tormenting myself, or admonishing me to make something happen. The narcissism of self-doubt can be really stifling and accepting that nobody was forcing me to do this cleared it right up. The story turned out garbage, but the advice is still true today.

Q **What advice would you tell your 21-year-old self, knowing what you know now?**

A Don't put stupid conditions on happiness; don't seek approval; try molly; buy clothes that fit.

" . . . a talented long-term writing group is the easiest way to get the feedback, encouragement, and deadlines you need to get through the rough early years. "

Tony Tulathimutte

Be comfortable being weird

Anne C. McClain

Astronaut

There is overachieving, and there is overachieving **ANNE C. McCLAIN**-style. In 2013, McClain and seven others were selected by NASA to train as astronauts — there were over 6,000 applicants, and she was the youngest to be chosen. Born in Spokane, Washington, McClain went east to enroll at West Point, where she earned a B.S. in mechanical/aeronautical engineering. She then spent two years in England on a Marshall Scholarship, and added a couple of masters degrees to her resume — she also practiced rugby, and got good enough to spend a few years on the U.S. national team, the Eagles, though the 2000s. McClain served 15 months in Operation Iraqi Freedom, flying 216 combat missions as pilot-in-command and Air Mission Commander. But all the while, space was calling; now 39, she's training to go up to the International Space Station in 2019.

Q **How old were you when you decided you wanted to be an astronaut?**

A I was about three years old. I probably watched some shuttle launches on TV. There was just something really inspiring about it. As I got older, there was always something very magical about seeing the space shuttle and astronauts doing space walks and things like that. I couldn't — and I still can't — put into words why that struck me. Maybe I felt it was like a destiny. A lot of times when I hear kids say they want to do something, I pay attention to how it makes them feel when they think about it, rather than try to get them to articulate exactly why they want to do something. I remember an interview with a mountain climber who was asked "Why do you do it?" And he said, "I finally came to understand that if somebody has to ask that question, they may never understand why I do it." That struck me because it was something that you felt rather than cognitively decided on.

Q **How did your family react to your interest?**

A They were very supportive. My mom always sees the

possibility where there may not be one. Even if she wasn't allowed to do something, she always felt like she would be able to at some point. She was very good at leading by example, of ignoring anything and anybody that said no, or that discouraged me, and really just focused on the possibilities. Also, you can be really unrealistic in your dreams but you have to be very realistic about your path. She knew my dream and she would always try to help me connect that to the reality of, "Yes, you need to study for your math test." I was pretty driven when I was younger, but at any point when I started to doubt myself or somebody else started doubting me, my mom was always there to remind me that I could do whatever I wanted as long as I worked for it.

Q Did you have a role model or a mentor when you were growing up?

A There was never one person that I ever thought I wanted to mold myself after. I think that actually worked out for me because whatever I was pursuing, I would see somebody who was really good at it and then I took the traits from them. It didn't matter what age or background they were or if they were the same gender. When I got in the military, I thought, "I want to be the best pilot I can be. Who are the senior-ranking people who are the most respected — that's who I want to model myself after?" That was really important for me because growing up there was not a lot of military people around me. In high school the teachers made all the difference. I found teachers that I thought were well-liked and tried to pay attention not only to why they taught really well but why people liked them.

When I was a senior at West Point I was awarded the Marshall Scholarship, which is for two years of graduate school in England. I had a few critical points in my career when I had mentors step in and really help me out, and that was one of them. The war in the Middle East had just kicked off and I had a huge sense of duty and responsibility that I needed to serve my country. I wanted to go straight into the military. But I had a mentor, a colonel at West Point, who said, "You are going to grad school. It seems like a long time right now, but it's really not, and you'll serve your country when you get back." That was one of the best things he said to me. I came back from grad school and went to flight school. So I did come back and serve.

Q Did you see West Point as a step toward your ultimate goal of being an astronaut?

A It kept all the doors open and opened a lot more doors on that path. I realized at an early age that with a goal like becoming an astronaut, you can control a lot of your path but you can't control that final selection. It's like a sprinter: They can control how fast they run but they can't control how fast everybody else runs. I recognized that very few people get selected and so it was important to choose a career that kept those doors open but that I would have wanted to do even if I wasn't selected.

Q **Were there any particular challenges or big breaks when you were in your late teens?**

A The biggest break was probably getting into West Point. I was so focused on it that I don't know what I would have done if I hadn't gotten in. I still would have pursued the military, for sure, the Army, the ROTC or something. I visited West Point when I was a senior in high school and there was this huge recognition of how hard it was going to be and how it wasn't going to be as fun as I'd pictured. There was probably a part of dread because I realized what it was going to be like, but I also knew I wanted to do it. It's such a critical age, between 18 and 23, 24. I think it's when the majority of people walk away from their dreams, saying, "Well, it was just a little kid's dream and now I need to do something more realistic." But people self-eliminate. And I always thought, "I'm not going to self-eliminate, I'm not going to stop going forward." I never made a decision that closed a door. That's what I always tell people in that age group, 18 to 23: Whatever your dream is, you can't select it today, you can't select it tomorrow, but what you can do is keep that door open and take steps forward on that path.

Q So it's a matter of putting as many assets on your side as possible?

A Absolutely. Many people I talk to say, "Wow, I could never have done that." And I think, "Yes, you could have done that — you chose not to when you made this decision. Maybe you dropped out of college, or you didn't challenge yourself to choose a hard major, or you dropped the class you thought you couldn't pass."

Q What's the NASA process?

A Every three to five years, NASA solicits applications for new astronaut classes, as needed. In fact, the first class since I was selected in 2013, is coming [in the summer of 2017]. Everybody is welcome to apply. They have an agreement with the military services so if they select a military astronaut, we remain on active duty and we're assigned at NASA. The class that's about to report had about 18,000 applications and only 12 were selected.

There's been a huge amount of interest in space flight again because of the commercial companies. And also because you see a lot of movies and books about space flight, and I think a lot more people are interested in it.

Q **Maybe it also has something to do with the fact that a manned mission to Mars seems more feasible?**

A Absolutely. And I think a lot of that realism is what's driving the pop-culture interest right now. It's interesting because the folks I've met in the new class either had applied before or have always wanted to be astronauts. I haven't met anybody in the new class yet that said "I saw this movie three years ago so I decided to apply." But I have to think this higher number of applicants has to do with more people being aware. NASA more than ever is such a powerful, unifying force. We work with people all over the world to accomplish a mission and I'm heartened by the number of applicants.

Q **Is there a lesson you've learned over the years that's been important to you?**

A Being comfortable outside of your comfort zone. A lot of high schoolers go visit college campuses and say, "I was really comfortable there, it just seemed to fit." But I think you should look for things that make you uncomfortable. The only way to get to dreams that seem really far away is to do things you've never done before, to take a chance and risk failure. If you're too comfortable with the next step, then it's probably not the right step if you're going for a big dream. I remember sitting on the airplane flying to West Point when I was 18 years old, and I was afraid I might not even make it through basic training. But every time you successfully get out of your comfort zone, the next time it's still scary but at least it's a familiar scary. Throughout my career I would hear about things and immediately think "I don't know if I can do that, I don't know if I'm good enough." My next thought was: "Well, I guess I've got to go try." I remember sitting on the plane going to Houston for my final astronaut interview and I had the exact same feelings as when I was 18 going to West Point. But I had challenged myself enough throughout my life that I knew I just had to put one foot in front of the other. To summarize all that: get out of your comfort zone because your dreams don't live in your comfort zone.

Q Do you remember your 21st birthday?

A I have a summer birthday so I was on leave. It wasn't that big of a deal. I'm not a partier and I wasn't then, I was a little more focused than that. It was low-key, I went out and celebrated with a couple of close friends.

Q **Knowing what you know now, what advice would you give your 21-year-old self?**

A When I started test-pilot school, I'd been told that all these other people were doing this and that, they had this background and that background, and my mom said, "Anne, you have always been successful to this point, so you need to not pay attention to what anybody else is doing and trust yourself." And that gave me a lot of peace. Don't take cues from people around you: At some point you're going to be so unique at what you're trying to do, the only person you have to rely on will be yourself. And you have to trust yourself that you're doing the right things. So maybe it would have given me some peace earlier to be reminded to trust myself.

When I played on the national rugby team, our coach said, "When you go out in your life and you are surrounded by people who don't have the same dream of playing on the national team, you're going to have to be comfortable being the weird one. You're going to be the weird one who gets up early and works out, you're going to be the weird one that's holding a different diet. But you're going to have to be the weird one if we're going to be successful as a national team." That speaks to the same thing: it's trusting yourself to pursue a dream.

"The only way to get to dreams that seem really far away is to do things you've never done before, to take a chance and risk failure. **"**

Anne C. McClain

Maintain an openness
to being wrong

Allison A. DeVito

Counsel in the Office of the
Air Force General Counsel

ALLISON A. DeVITO, Counsel in the Office of the Air Force General Counsel, is proof that change can come from the inside. As a member of the Air Force Judge Advocate General's Corps (JAG Corps), she provided legal and policy advice to commanders and senior leaders. As chief of the Victim Issues and Policy Branch, Military Justice Division, Air Force Legal Operations Agency, DeVito, 36, was instrumental in developing policies on sexual abuse and implementing legal representation for its victims in the Air Force. When she served in Afghanistan as Rule of Law Field Support Officer, she mentored 30 Afghan judges and prosecutors, and worked on shoring up the local judicial system. A recipient of a 2015-2016 Outstanding Young Military Lawyer Award, DeVito went to Notre Dame and the Fordham School of Law.

Q Did you have a role model growing up? If yes, who was it and why?

A My parents were (and still are) without a doubt my greatest role models. They both achieved professional success in demanding fields, while always being available and present as parents. Their work ethic is unmatched and I admire their ability to prioritize our family while still progressing professionally. They gave me a tremendous amount of latitude to try different things, from sports and music to the wide range of extracurricular activities (Princeton Model Congress, Ohio Girls State, summer programs that took me to Washington, D.C., Australia and New Zealand) that I participated in throughout high school. Notably, I was completely average (or below average) at a number of these things (I ran for Student Council and lost and was never fast enough for the Varsity Cross Country team, but still had fun on the Junior Varsity squad), but they were always supportive and never discouraged me from trying new things.

Q **Who or what influenced you in your teens/early adulthood?**

A My biggest motivation during that time was to achieve "success" — which generally for me meant academic success. While my parents' success motivated me, I think I was largely self-driven in this regard and fortunate to be surrounded by peers who were also driven and ambitious.

I was also very motivated to try different things and live in different places. There was no set goal in mind — I did not set off for college knowing what profession I would like, where I would like to live, or certainly how much money I would like to make. We lived in Ohio and in fact my No. 1 criteria for attending college was that I leave Ohio. Even though ultimately that meant going right next door to Indiana! I came home and worked in my hometown the first summer after college (two jobs — at a restaurant and a mom-and-pop sports store). From then on I sought out different internships and job opportunities that seemed interesting: internship for Catholic Charities in southern California; internships for the Department of Labor and Department of Justice in Washington, D.C.; co-founder of the Student Hurricane Network at Fordham Law School, to name a few. Looking at my résumé in those years as I came out of law school, employers would be unlikely to see a specific path. I simply sought out opportunities that seemed new, interesting, and where I might be able to contribute. The desire to live/work in different places was a big motivator, as was a desire to work in public service, either for the government, non-profits, or international organizations.

Q What illuminating, instructive and/or inspirational thoughts can you share that reflect your perspective on that time of your life?

A I had a tremendous amount of freedom during that time in my life to take risks and see where hard work would lead. And I would encourage any young person to do the same. There is a lot of value in trying something and failing, or trying something and deciding you don't like it and would rather do something else. Particularly with the pace at which the global economy is changing, the ability to adapt and refresh your skills to reinvent your career I think will become even more important.

An important caveat is that I had tremendous financial support from my parents, who paid for my college and law-school tuition, and living expenses. The vast majority of young people are not nearly as fortunate and many have financial responsibilities (to their family or student loans) that impact their career decisions. It's also much easier to say that either "money doesn't matter" or is not the deciding factor in selecting job opportunities when you have never wanted for money in your life. So I don't judge those who seek big paychecks right out of school or for whom that is a significant motivator. Nonetheless, I would encourage young people to take reasonable risks in the pursuit of meaningful work. From 18 to 26 I lived somewhere different every summer between school years, with countless roommates and living situations along the way, moving frequently with just a couple suitcases. Having limited personal responsibilities provides one flexibility in taking advantage of opportunities as they arise.

Q **What was your biggest challenge or biggest break in your teens/early adulthood that led you to where you are today?**

A My biggest challenge during that time was to maintain resiliency and keep moving forward through what I would now acknowledge are routine setbacks (but seemed like a much bigger deal at the time). I had turned down the job offer that followed my second year of law school summer (because the three-year commitment seemed like such a long time!) and did not have a job lined up once I took the bar exam. Fortuitously I landed a clerkship at the International Criminal Tribunal for Rwanda and the former Yugoslavia. I decided to move to D.C. from there with the goal of landing a job on Capitol Hill. Frankly, I thought my clerkship was pretty cool and that I had good credentials overall. So I was a little surprised at how hard I had to work to land a job. I hit the networking game hard and was fortunate at the number of alumni connections and others that I contacted cold who were willing to meet with me (while I was working as an attorney doing very mundane document review for various law firms). But I still had to work as an unpaid intern for a number of months for a Member of Congress before landing a paid position in her office (a typical path for gaining entry-level employment on Capitol Hill), and that was a tough period in terms of my confidence in my own abilities.

Q **Looking back, what motivated you to get to where you are now?**

A I ended up leaving the job on Capitol Hill after only a year to join the Air Force JAG Corps for a couple of reasons. The practical one was that I was two years out of law school and knew that if I wanted to be a practicing attorney the door would soon close to gaining that type of experience. The other was what I like to think was a little humility. Working on Capitol Hill can be a heady place as a young person and I had a decent amount of self-awareness that I really didn't know much about the world. So I wanted an opportunity to work issues on the ground that I was ultimately interested in from a policy perspective.

 What were your dreams in your late teens/early twenties?
 I didn't have specific dreams at that time other than to continue to learn and be successful academically and in the jobs that I had. I really enjoyed working in public service and continued to pursue that path.

 Could you picture what you would end up doing, or not at all?
 Not at all. My grandfather served in the Air Force, but it was not a topic of conversation in our relationship growing up and I did not live in an area with a lot of military influence. And it was never something I considered as a career path until much later after law school.

 When did you first realize you were into/good at what you do now?
 I have not loved every job that I have had — which has been good in that I know what type of job I can succeed at and what opportunities to keep seeking out. The jobs have all varied so much that it's hard to pinpoint a realization of being good or interested in something. I can say that I realized that I thrived in fast paced work environments working on high profile issues for demanding bosses. I also

do my best work in jobs that are constantly changing. The Air Force JAG Corps has been a fantastic fit for me because the very nature of our career path requires moving to a new job generally every two or three years, so there is truly never an opportunity to become bored.

Q Were your family and/or friends encouraging?

A Yes, my family and friends have always been incredibly supportive. I am also fortunate to have friends and family members that are successful in a wide range of occupations, offering a great perspective in comparing career paths, different opportunities, and the pros and cons to the routes we have all taken.

Q What was school like? A lot of people say high school or college was a turning point. Did you feel that way?

A I have not felt that there was a particular turning point for me. Mostly I have felt that my career has been on a steady trajectory, continuing to learn more and have more responsibility with each successive position.

Q Do you remember your 21st birthday? Was it a big deal or just like any birthday?

A I do remember my 21st birthday, partially because I was one of the last of my group of college friends to turn 21 so it was kind of a "finally!" moment. But even then it wasn't a particularly big deal. It was at the start of my senior year of college so more a marker of the start of figuring out what to do with the next stage of my life.

Q Do you have a favorite quote or mantra that keeps you going?

A I don't necessarily have a favorite quote or mantra. When faced with adversity or particular situations or periods in my life that have felt tough, I try to just keep moving and take things one day at a time. In the military the course of an officer's career typically takes them from working at the tactical to the strategic level. I think I have always had a bit more of a strategic mindset and ability to focus on the big picture and I try to keep that perspective in mind, which suits me well in temperament and style in both my day to day work and long term professional outlook.

Q What lesson have you learned over the years that has stuck with you?

A The greatest lesson is that there are new lessons to be learned every day, from everyone, and to maintain an openness to "being wrong," seeing different perspectives, and adjusting your views on issues or approach to resolving certain situations.

Q **What advice would you tell your 21-year-old self, knowing what you know now?**

A I have no regrets about the decisions I made as a 21-year-old or the decisions I have made since. When thinking about the path I have taken, I typically mark my college choice as the first decision almost wholly within my control that set me on the path to where I am today and where I might go in the future. A different college choice would have yielded different opportunities and so on and so forth. I have learned so much and worked with fantastic people in every job I have had, from selling chocolates at the Godiva store in Union Station to being deployed with the Army in Afghanistan, and everything in between. As a result I would tell a 21-year-old to make the best informed decision they can at the time and then not look back. If something doesn't work out, there will be more opportunities down the road. You just have to keep moving forward.

" . . . I have always had a bit more of a strategic mindset and the ability to focus on the big picture and I try to keep that perspective in mind . . . "

Allison A. DeVito

Be your best and you'll handle the rest

Tamika Catchings

WNBA All-Star & Olympic Gold Medalist

Basketball runs in the Catchings family: Dad Harvey Lee played in the NBA from 1974 to 1985, and daughter **TAMIKA CATCHINGS** was a shining star of the WNBA from 2002 to 2016 — the last four years as president of the players association. But even before going pro, young Tamika made her mark: She scored an elusive quintuple-double (25 points, 18 rebounds, 11 assists, 10 steals and 10 blocks) in high school, then played with the legendary coach Pat Summitt at the University of Tennessee. She was drafted by the Indiana Fever, where she spent her entire American career as a small forward. In addition to leading the league in rebounding and steals, Catchings won a WNBA championship and four Olympic gold medals with the U.S. team. Now 37 and retired, she continues to be involved with the Pacers organization's front office as Director of Player Programs and Franchise Development.

Q Did you have a role model growing up?

A My role models growing up have always been my parents. I was born with a hearing impairment, so grew up a little insecure in who I was. My parents always were there to push me to new heights and encourage me to go after my dreams. Outside of my family, my basketball idol was Alonzo Mourning. I loved Zo because when I watched him play he just seemed like he could do everything well. Whatever his team needed, he could provide and I admired and respected that about him.

Q Who or what influenced you in your teens/early adulthood?

A I always just wanted to fit in, personally, when I was younger. By the time I was into my teens, basketball became a priority for me, but I always wanted to help people. Pat Summitt came into my life at that time, and it was her who showed me how to be an athlete, but still have the time and make the effort to be a good person and a contributor in the community. She was my coach, but she became my mentor and my friend.

Q **What illuminating, instructive and/or inspirational thoughts can you share that reflect your perspective on that time of your life?**

A "I can do all things through Christ who strengthens me" is a Bible verse that I live by a lot. My family spent a lot of time in church when I was young. There were times when I first went to college that I didn't always attend church, but I still believed. I strengthened my faith again through adversity and a slight nudge from God. I think that verse says everything for me.

Q **What was your your biggest challenge or biggest break in your teens/early adulthood that led you to where you are today?**

A Outside of my parents getting divorced when I was in the sixth grade, there were two big challenges I faced. The first was in between my sophomore and junior year of high school when my mom and I moved to Texas. The second was when I went to college at the University of Tennessee. In both situations, I had to learn to communicate on my own, and live on my own, and develop new friendships. I had always been pretty shy and self-conscious because of my hearing and speech difficulties as a little girl. Those two times helped and forced me to realize I could make it on my own, too.

Q Looking back, what motivated you?

A At first, it was just the discipline and drive to "fit in" and be normal every day at school as a young girl. But after that I think my faith was a big factor in continuing to drive myself. Even now, I am still motivated but instead of trying to be the best basketball player, I strive to have the biggest impact that I can in whatever it is I'm doing.

Q What were your dreams in your late teens/early twenties?

A Playing basketball. I set a goal in the seventh grade to play in the NBA, because my dad played in the NBA. But then my freshman year of college, the WNBA was established and I thought the league was created just for me!

Q Could you picture what you would end up doing?

A I knew that whatever I would do in life would be around sports (basketball especially). In what capacity I didn't know, but I loved the game of basketball and just all of the opportunities and doors that it has opened.

Q When did you first realize you were into/good at what you do now?

A So far as playing basketball, I realized I was good as a little girl. It was playing basketball that I realized if I practiced real hard, and was better than everybody else, even the boys, I couldn't get picked on. When I struggled and wanted to fit in, I went to the basketball court. I was always one of the first players picked for games, and I knew I belonged.

Q **Were your family and/or friends encouraging?**

A My family and friends were always encouraging. It's crazy because my dad told me when I was a youngster "You pick your friends, don't let your friends pick you." From that, the friends that were around me knew my passions and knew the goals I had set for myself. They were a part of my journey.

Q **What was school like? A lot of people say high school or college was a turning point. Did you feel that way?**

A Especially when I was young, school was hard for me. I was a good learner and took school seriously and got good grades, but I struggled socially and just wanted to fit in. I worked so hard, though, that I was good in school. I think, as a young woman, I really gained confidence when I got to college. My relationship with my teammates and Coach Summitt really helped me believe all that I could do, even outside of basketball.

Q **Do you remember your 21st birthday? Was it a big deal or just like any birthday?**

A Funny thing is, I don't remember my 21st birthday. I was definitely playing in the WNBA, and since my birthday is in the middle of the season, we could have been playing, traveling or Lord knows where I was. I guess that's a good thing LOL.

Q What advice would you give your 21-year-old self, knowing what you know now?

A I would say the same advice that I've lived by and that Pat kind of preached: "Always go 100 percent and stay true to yourself." I do believe that with that mindset, no matter what type of fame you experience, you'll always be prepared for life ahead.

" At first, it was just the discipline and drive to 'fit in' and be normal every day at school as a young girl. But after that I think my faith was a big factor in continuing to drive myself. Even now, I am still motivated but instead of trying to be the best basketball player, I strive to have the biggest impact that I can in whatever it is I'm doing. "

Tamika Catchings

Work hard. Show up.
Never give up!

Jeff M. Poulin

Arts Education Advocate

When he was two, **JEFF M. POULIN** started taking tap-dancing lessons. At 16, the young Maine native won a national competition put on by Dancers Inc. Now 27, Poulin is still very much involved in the arts — but as an advocate and educator rather than a dancer. As Arts Education Program Manager at the national advocacy organization, Americans for the Arts, he empowers and trains arts advocates nationwide, and speaks to all kinds of individuals and groups.

Poulin earned a Bachelor of Science in Entertainment Business from Oklahoma City University and a Master's in arts management and cultural policy from University College Dublin. Now he travels the country to talk about why the arts matter — pretty cool!

Q Did you have a role model growing up? If yes, who was it and why?

A I had many role models growing up. The communities from which I came clearly believed in empowering young people to follow their passion and drive towards their goals. In the theatre community, dance community and youth empowerment community, I found myself surrounded by adults who believed in me and encouraged me to pursue my passions for community organizing, policy change and performing on the stage.

Q Who or what influenced you in your teens/early adulthood?

A I always had an inherent passion for identifying injustice and working to correct it, whether this was in the hallways at school or in the systems of our country. I always looked up to my father who started his own business, but was simultaneously involved with community-based nonprofit organizations, serving as President of his local Kiwanis Club and contributing to the betterment of our community. This vision for change encouraged me to go down a career path where I could marry my passion for creativity and culture, alongside my drive for social change — and get paid to do it, too. I am very lucky that, today, I find myself in a place where all of those things have come together.

Q **What illuminating, instructive and/or inspirational thoughts can you share that reflect your perspective on that time of your life?**

A Go on adventures, take risks, meet interesting people, and seek to improve your world. Throughout my early life, I had the privilege of seeing the country and the world through numerous adventures in the performing arts world, met tons of interesting people and learned from their experiences, took risks and followed my heart, and ultimately was able to leverage those learning experiences, the network of connections and my self-confidence to go after my goals of making the world a better place.

Q **What was your biggest challenge or biggest break in your teens/early adulthood that led you to where you are today?**

A I remember, at one point, I was faced with several options — a metaphorical fork in my road. I went to the beach, weighed the pros and cons, spent time with friends and family to discuss the impacts of the decisions, and ultimately followed what my heart was telling me to do. This is how I performed on my first New York City stage and won a national dance title. The same scenario happened with college, and with opportunities immediately following college. Growing up in a coastal town in southern Maine, for me the key was always being surrounded by friends and family, truly thinking through the decision, and never underestimating the clarity afforded by staring out at the sea.

Q **Looking back, what motivated you to get to where you are now?**

A Witnessing injustice fueled my passion to dream big, work hard, and be where I needed to be to realize my vision. Working now as an advocate for arts education and creative learning for students — I was fueled by the injustice I saw in equity and access to learning opportunities in the arts for young people around the country. I grew up in a very privileged community with incredible opportunities to learn in and through the arts. Around the rest of the United States, I witnessed gigantic disparities between my community and that of the young people with whom I worked. It wasn't right — it still isn't right. But today, I have the distinct privilege to tackle policy initiatives, funding streams and public awareness of the inequities I witnessed a decade ago.

Q **What were your dreams in your late teens/early twenties?**

A Growing up in the arts — starting tap dance lessons at age two and community theater at age six — I always wanted to perform on Broadway. Later in my teens, I decided I wanted to produce Broadway shows. After performing around the country in my teens and producing shows in my early twenties, I realized that I was less passionate about making art, and more passionate about providing opportunity for others to make art, critique society, contribute to their communities and grow as people. I was afforded those opportunities to pursue my dreams, and now it is my time to step aside and do everything I can to enable others to achieve theirs.

Q **Could you picture what you would end up doing, or not at all?**

A I was largely unaware that there was a profession in what I do today. I always had the passion for this work and was honing my skills in my teens, but didn't know I could combine the passion and skills and get paid for it, until I got this job. It's truly a dream job: one day, I work with artists on how to be advocates in their community, the next day I attend a briefing on Capitol Hill, and the next day I see young people perform their art at the White House — it's incredible!

Q **When did you first realize you were into/good at what you do now?**

A When I lived in New York City, I realized very quickly that though I was good at it, I didn't want to hustle to make shows in order for a larger company to make money. I had several moments of clarity when I realized that I loved working with artists and young people so they could perform or make art to enable communities to heal, inspire, learn, or make a place their own. During my time living in Europe, I learned a lot about policy-making and research and found myself pursuing several opportunities working on initiatives that accomplished what I had realized was my goal: equity in access to the arts.

Q **Were your family and/or friends encouraging?**

A My family has always been supportive of me pursuing my dreams. My friends are often in the arts. They weren't surprised I ended up down this path, but many, like me, didn't realize it could be a full time job — so I had a bit of explaining to do.

Q **What was school like? A lot of people say high school or college was a turning point. Did you feel that way?**

A In high school, I was provided a number of opportunities to learn what I wanted to do and what I didn't want to do. In college, I found myself among my tribe of people;

constantly inspired by those who surrounded me. I look back and think of those with whom I am still connected and realize that we were all on the same journey towards our passions — the amount of success among my friends in numerous sectors of business, politics, arts, education, and the like — they always inspire me and keep me going.

Q Do you remember your 21st birthday? Was it a big deal or just like any birthday?

A It was definitely a big deal. I spent my birthday in rehearsals all day and then surrounded by people who loved me at midnight. Though it was an incredibly busy and stressful time in my life, my friends made me stop, breathe and take a moment of pure fun!

Q Do you have a favorite quote or mantra that keeps you going?

A "Never doubt that a small group of thoughtful, committed citizens can change the world. Indeed, it is the only thing that ever has." — Margaret Mead. I first heard this quote as a young person and it has consistently reassured me to keep trying to impact my world as best I can even when it feels impossible or if I feel alone.

Q What lesson have you learned over the years that has stuck with you?

A Learn a lot. Work hard. Show up. And never give up. These are lessons I began learning through the arts and have continued into my life in the political and education spheres. One must always learn as much as they can; and never stop learning. One must always work hard and put their best into every project they pursue. One must always show up to things and be present. And one must never give up, regardless of how challenging the feat is.

Q **What advice would you tell your 21-year-old self, knowing what you know now?**

A Surround yourself with people who will challenge you to be better. When situations seem hard or even impossible, they are usually worth it. Listen to your heart and your elders for advice. Take risks. Give back to the communities from which you came. Always keep pushing forward to be better.

---

66 It's truly a dream job: one day, I work with artists on how to be advocates in their community, the next day I attend a briefing on Capitol Hill, and the next day I see young people perform their art at the White House — it's incredible! 99

Jeff Poulin

About the Commissioning Editor

Elisabeth Vincentelli is a freelance writer and editor based in Brooklyn, New York. Her résumé includes stints as arts and entertainment editor at *Time Out New York* and chief theater critic at *The New York Post*. She regularly contributes to *The New York Times*, *The New Yorker*, *Newsday*, *The Village Voice*, *CNN Travel* and *Slate*; her work has also appeared in *The Los Angeles Times*, *Rolling Stone*, *Entertainment Weekly* and *Salon*. Elisabeth has written the books *ABBA Gold* and *ABBA Treasures*, as well as liner notes for a reissue of the compilation *ABBA Gold*. Her essay "Bulgarian Idol" was featured in the anthology *Best Music Writing of 2009*. She is a regular guest and co-host on the syndicated TV show *Theater Talk*.

Credits